12/19/12

The SECRET GOSPEL of IRELAND

The SECRET

GOSPEL of

IRELAND

THE UNTOLD STORY OF HOW SCIENCE
AND DEMOCRACY DESCENDED FROM A
REMARKABLE FORM OF CHRISTIANITY
THAT DEVELOPED IN ANCIENT IRELAND

JAMES BEHAN & LEO BEHAN

ISBN 978-0-985458317 (hc.)
ISBN 978-0-985458300 (pbk.)
ISBN 978-0-985458324 (ebk.)

Library of Congress Control Number: 2012906136

www.secretgospelofireland.com

Skywest Publishing
Seattle, Washington

May the road rise to meet you,
May the wind be always at your back.
May the sun shine warm upon your face,
The rains fall soft upon your fields.
And until we meet again,
May God hold you in the palm of his hand.

—*Traditional Irish Blessing*

CONTENTS

INTRODUCTION

On a clear day in the year AD 82, the Roman general Gnaeus Julius Agricola stood on the windswept coast of Britain and cast his gaze across the Irish Sea. He had just conquered most of Britain for Rome and now he set his sights on Ireland. His son-in-law, the Roman historian Tacitus, wrote, "I have often heard him say that a single legion with a few auxiliaries could conquer and occupy Ireland, and that it would have a salutary effect on Britain for the Roman arms to be seen everywhere, and for freedom, so to speak, to be banished from its sight." But no Roman army would ever set foot on the Emerald Isle. At the height of its power, the Roman Empire would stretch as far west as Britain. But it would never conquer and occupy Ireland. Every time some Roman planned to take Ireland, the troops were needed in other parts of the empire to repel barbarians or crush a rebellion or quell a riot. The empire simply couldn't spare a single legion for what seemed like such a minor gain. And so the ancient Irish continued living as they always had, free of Roman rule, until, just forty-five years before the fall of Rome in 476, a different sort of Roman came ashore. Not a soldier, but a Roman Catholic bishop.

His name was Palladius, and in the year 431, he was sent by the Church in Rome to convert the Irish to Christianity. It was an unprecedented event! It was the first time the Church launched a mission to spread Christianity beyond the borders of the Roman Empire. Indeed, the Irish were the only people ever to receive Christianity directly from the ancient Romans without first being conquered and occupied by Rome.

The coming together of Rome and Ireland in the fifth century is an event that has never been fully appreciated in the long history of Western civilization. Of course everyone knows about St. Patrick, the great patron saint of Ireland to whom millions of people hoist a beer each March 17. But Patrick wasn't Irish. He was Roman; or more accurately, he was a Romano-Briton. He was a descendant of the Romans and native Celts who had intermixed during the four hundred years that Rome had occupied Britain. And, following in the footsteps of Palladius, he went to Ireland to spread Christianity just as the Roman Empire was crumbling.

As history well records, the Western Roman Empire finally collapsed in 476 and civilization in Europe receded for a very long time. For most people today, the next thousand years or so of European history is a bit of a blur. It comes wrapped in terms like "Dark Ages" and "Middle Ages" and "medieval." By most accounts, it was a middle period between the ancient and the modern, a vast intellectual desert that stretched between the fall of Rome at the one end and the Renaissance at the other. It was a time of heroes like King Arthur and his knights, a time of unicorns and faeries, of wizards and dragons, of Vikings and monks, of myths and seemingly endless fodder for Hollywood movies and children's books. It was a time when the real and the imaginary shared the same space in the minds of men. And perhaps most cynically, it was a time of bondage to the gloom and superstition of religious belief: a time before science and reason liberated the West from blind faith, the fetters of ignorance, and those who would seek to exploit faith and ignorance for wealth and power. Or was it?

The tree is known by its fruit. But what are the fruits of Western civilization? The two greatest advances of the modern West—science and democracy—seem completely foreign to the world of our medieval ancestors. And their way of thinking seems completely alien to the modern mind. They explained natural phenomena by resorting to supernatural causes. Natural disasters like floods and forest fires were often interpreted as the wrath of God or the work of the Devil. Moreover, they had no concept of the sovereignty of the individual or natural rights. They believed God ordained kings to protect men from themselves and each other. Thus some men were born to rule while others were born to serve.

When pressed to name a single thing from the Middle Ages that advanced human progress, most people today would probably be at a loss. The entire epoch seems marked by monasticism, pilgrimages, warring kingdoms, serfdom, the Black Death, the Inquisition, and the Crusades. So it's no wonder why Renaissance and modern thinkers saw no connection between themselves and their medieval predecessors. After all, Renaissance and modern thinkers made tremendous gains for Western civilization by explaining the world according to natural causes, not supernatural ones. They engineered the first dome in Europe (the Duomo in Florence, Italy) since the ancient Romans built the Pantheon. And, eventually, they planted the seed of today's modern democracies with the idea that government is a social contract instituted among men instead of a divine office ordained by God.

The thinkers of the Renaissance and the modern age felt they had more in common with the ancient Greeks and Romans than with medieval Europeans. The ancient Greeks and Romans had things that medieval Europeans never had like toilets and plumbing. The ancient Greeks had democracy, philosophy, mathematics, advanced architecture, poetry, drama, and naturalistic art. The ancient Romans had a republic before they had an empire, and theirs was the most technologically advanced civilization of their age producing such wonders as the Roman aqueducts, the Colosseum, and the Pantheon. Compared to the Greco-Roman world, medieval Europe looked primitive. All of which led Europeans to see the explosion of ideas and culture during the Renaissance and modern age as originating with a rebirth of ideas from classical antiquity instead of as the fruit of medieval European culture. Even the word Renaissance means rebirth.

Yet this narrative raises more questions than it answers. For example, why did Europeans suddenly develop an intense interest in all things Greek and Roman? Throughout the Middle Ages, European scholars studied the greatest minds of Greece and Rome and were well versed in the philosophy, literature, and art of the ancient world. The fruits of Greco-Roman civilization were never really lost, so what explains this sudden rebirth of ideas a thousand years later? Why haven't we looked to the centuries immediately preceding the Renaissance for answers instead of leapfrogging all the way back to antiquity? But perhaps the biggest fly in the ointment is Christianity. For almost a millennium before the Renaissance, the dominant force in the lives of nearly every man, woman, and child in Western Europe came to be the Christian faith. And yet Christianity has been all but ignored in the story of how our modern world developed. Does it make any sense at all that this pillar of civilization didn't have a tremendous influence on what came next? Does it make any sense at all that a thousand years of European history has simply been written off as the Middle Ages? How did Western civilization really develop?

The answer lies hidden in Ireland. The coming together of Rome and Ireland in the fifth century happened on the cusp of two great epochs—the Roman and the European. As the Western Roman Empire collapsed in Britain and on the continent, Christian Ireland was just being born. Yet Ireland had never been part of Roman civilization like its neighbors Britain and Gaul. Thus in Ireland, Christianity would be left to mix with Ireland's own unique culture, which was very different from that of Rome. And that's where the Romans perhaps misjudged an ancient people and their little Emerald Isle in the sea. Because just as Rome came together with Ireland in the fifth century, a new Christian Ireland would come together with a post-Roman Europe beginning in the sixth century. But while the Romans intended for Christianity to change the Irish, they gave little thought to how the Irish might change Christianity and, in time, all of Western civilization.

CHAPTER ONE

How an African Bishop Invented Europe

n *April 30*, in the year AD 418, the Roman Empire was in decline. The Roman people no longer shared the beliefs of their forefathers who had built the empire. Indeed, by the year 418, the empire had too many different kinds of people with too many different kinds of beliefs to sustain Roman civilization. Now, in the absence of a common purpose, there was nothing to rally all the different people against the government corruption, barbarian invasions, crime, and the steep decline in public morals that would inevitably destroy the empire in little more than fifty years. Rome was falling one stone at a time, only the people didn't know it. Nobody realized that the Roman Empire had been built by harnessing the selfish desires of men for a common purpose—to dominate the world. Nobody, that is, except for an African bishop named Augustine.

For many years, Augustine had waged a battle of ideas against an Irish monk named Pelagius. But this wasn't just any battle of ideas. These ideas had the power to transform civilizations. These ideas had the power to give mankind a new purpose and a new civilization. On April 30, 418, after followers of the Irishman rioted in Rome, the emperor resolved to settle the score between Augustine and Pelagius once and for all. It was one of the most important decisions a man has ever made. The emperor was about to condemn Pelagius and make Augustine's ideas on God and man the law. He was about to alter the course of human history in ways no man had ever dared to imagine. A new civilization was coming.

Aurelius Augustinus, or Augustine, was born on November 13, 354, in the African town of Thagaste. Today, Thagaste is the town of Souk Ahras, Algeria. The province that the Romans named Africa occupied a relatively small area of land that now cuts across northeastern Algeria, northern Tunisia, and the western coast of Libya. And from the Mediterranean coast looking north, Roman Africa faced Sicily. The native people who lived in this region were called Afri. The Romans formed an adjective by adding the Latin suffix *ca* and called the land *Africa*, a name that later came to describe the entire continent. The Afri had light skin, fair hair, and were probably European in origin. Augustine himself was a Berber, which are an indigenous, light-skinned people of North Africa.

Although the journey from Rome to Africa took only a few days by ship, Africa was a very different world from Rome. Whereas Rome was a cosmopolitan mix of people and ideas, Africa was seen by many Romans as a cultural backwater. It had long been important to the empire for its agriculture. Commonly called the granary of Rome, Africa fed the Eternal City by exporting grain and olive oil. Life in Africa was difficult for most, even brutal. The small towns and the agricultural estates they served were ruled by men who were more like mafia godfathers than landlords, and the peasant farmers who worked the land were their serfs. The lives of these peasant farmers were marked by servitude, hunger, beatings, and extreme poverty with little hope of doing better. Their surplus harvests went to their Roman-African landlords for export. But they could at least be grateful for not being one of the many slaves in Africa that lived at the pleasure of their masters while toiling as domestic servants and field laborers.

Augustine, however, was neither a peasant nor a slave. He was born a Roman citizen. Augustine's mother was a devout Roman Catholic named Monica. She was born to an affluent, Roman Catholic family in Thagaste around the year 331. By all accounts, she was a well-behaved and obedient daughter, except for an incident involving the family wine cellar. As a girl, Monica began to steal sips of her parents' wine. Soon she found herself stealing entire cups of wine and getting drunk. She thought no one was looking until one day she was shamed by a slave girl. One of the family's slave girls, a girl who was about Monica's own age, saw what she was doing and mocked her for her gluttony. And having been shamed by a slave, Monica never drank again.

Monica married a pagan named Patricius while she was perhaps still in her teens. Patricius, on the other hand, wasn't in his teens. He was closer to forty. Like most Roman marriages, their marriage was arranged by their families. But even with an arranged marriage, Monica couldn't choose her in-laws. She got off to a bad start with her mother-in-law because some of the family's slaves had spread rumors that Monica didn't like Patricius' mother. When Patricius' mother discovered what the slaves had done, she demanded Patricius punish them. So Patricius gave each a beating and harmony was restored.

Patricius was a decurion, which was a civil servant that acted as city councilor and tax collector. Despite his lofty title, Patricius wasn't rich. He owned a small amount of land and held a modest number of slaves. Together, he and Monica had at least three children. Monica gave birth to Augustine when she was twenty-three years old. Augustine had at least one brother named Navigius, who was likely his elder; and he had at least one sister whose name and age are lost to history.

Although Patricius was a pagan, Monica was determined to raise Augustine and his siblings in the Catholic faith. She devoted herself entirely to her children, praying for them constantly and teaching them the Christian virtues of faith, hope, and love. She wanted desperately for her children to be baptized, but Patricius always said no. He finally consented to Augustine's baptism when his son became gravely ill and it looked as though he might die. We can just imagine Monica, this devoutly Catholic mother, pleading with her pagan husband to allow her dying little boy to be baptized. Fortunately for the family, Augustine survived. And in turn, Patricius canceled the baptism.

Patricius revered his wife, but he was far from an ideal husband. He cheated on Monica and he had a violent temper. He almost certainly beat his children. The abuse must have been hell for Augustine and his siblings, the terror and shame of the beatings, the unbearable guilt of watching their mother cry for her children as though this pageant of blood and tears was somehow their fault. Yet of all the husbands and fathers in Thagaste, Patricius was one of the best. He could, at times, be very generous with Monica. Moreover, unlike almost every other husband in town, he never beat his wife. This was so uncommon that the other wives would come to Monica with their bruised faces and bloodied lips for advice on how not to get beaten by their husbands. She half-jokingly told them to keep their mouths shut when their husbands were in a bad mood.

Augustine grew to despise his father, and in later years, he praised Monica for striving to make God his father rather than Patricius. Nevertheless, it was Patricius who was responsible for Augustine's education. An education was an expensive and uncommon luxury in those days. Patricius took great pride in being able to send his son to school, first sending his son to school in their hometown of Thagaste and then to Madaura, a university town some twenty miles away. Unfortunately, the money ran out when Augustine was sixteen years old.

Augustine was forced to drop out of school because Patricius, who had always given to Augustine's education without question or complaint, could no longer afford to pay. Without school to occupy his mind, Augustine spent a rotten year in Thagaste getting into trouble, even stealing. It looked like Augustine might be headed for a life of crime until a wealthy friend of the family intervened, a man named Romanianus. Romanianus paid for Augustine to attend the rhetoric schools at Carthage, which was located on the Mediterranean coast, about 150 miles northeast of Thagaste. Carthage was the Western Empire's second largest city. If Rome was New York, then Carthage was Chicago.

For Augustine, going away to Carthage was the Roman equivalent of going off to college. And what kind of young man was Augustine when he headed off to college in the big city at the age of seventeen? He was his parents' son, which is to say he was a Christian soul in a pagan body. If Monica embodied the Christian virtues of faith, hope, and love, then Patricius embodied the pagan virtues of worldly power, domination, and glory. Whereas Monica was humble and spiritual, Patricius was proud and physical. Patricius even took note of the increased size of Augustine's genitals one day at the public baths. Apparently, he saw it as an auspicious prognosticator of grandchildren and found joy in telling it to Augustine's mother. Like any adolescent boy, Augustine was humiliated. One can only speculate as to how much Monica and Patricius affected Augustine's choices as an adult. But soon, while away at school in Carthage, Augustine would attempt to embrace the world of the spirit and reject the world of the flesh by joining a cult.

It was also around this time that Augustine developed his infamous addiction to sex. Every saint begins as a sinner, and Augustine's favorite sin was lust. In modern parlance, he was a sex addict. And he knew it. He came to see his sexual appetite as an uncontrollable alter ego that was at war with his spirit. His sex drive was like another person inside of him that sinned against his will, a kind of Dr. Jekyll and Mr. Hyde. Eventually, he would become a walking contradiction—a proud intellectual with a tremendous libido who despised his body. And in about fifteen years, this internal conflict between his body and his soul would produce the most famous spiritual conversion the world has ever known. But that was yet to come.

Augustine moved to Carthage in 371 and did what any young man might do his first time away from home: he got drunk, had sex, experimented with new philosophies and religions, and generally took in everything the big city had to offer. He had been a prodigal son in Carthage for about a year when tragedy befell his family. His father Patricius died. If Augustine grieved for Patricius, he never mentioned it. And if Patricius comes across as an unloving brute all too often, it's because the only source for information about his life is Augustine. Yet Patricius wasn't beyond redemption, even for his son. Near the end of his life, after all was said and done, this old pagan who was Augustine's father finally opened his heart to his wife's faith, hope, and love and became a Christian.

In the same year that his father died, Augustine met a woman and took her as his concubine. He took a concubine, not a wife. Augustine's ambitions stopped him from taking a wife. He knew that if he took a wife at his young age, he would be stuck in Thagaste like his father. And by waiting until he was more successful, he knew he could marry a woman of a higher social status. So he took a concubine.

Taking a concubine was a common practice in the Roman Empire. It was a cheaper and easier alternative to a full marriage. A full marriage was a terribly complex affair that had to be arranged by the families of a man and woman of the same social class. Concubinage, on the other hand, was a kind of lesser union recognized by the law. But it was less than ideal, especially for women. Men often abandoned their concubines for wives. Upgrading from a concubine to a wife was seen as a sign of moral improvement. A legitimate marriage was always preferable to anything less. A concubine was never respected like a wife. She was there for sex and to cook and clean and to look after children, in that order. In ancient Rome, women belonged to men either as daughters, wives, widows, slaves, or something in between.

Augustine and his concubine are one of history's tragic love stories. They were together for some thirteen years, from 372 to 385. In the year 373, about a year after they met, she gave birth to Augustine's son. They named their son Adeodatus, a name that meant gift of God. Augustine never revealed his concubine's name in his writings and, in many ways, came to regard her as part of his licentious past. Perhaps he associated her name with his sex addiction. Ultimately, Augustine was forced to abandon his concubine when his mother arranged a full marriage for him. Years later he recalled their parting when he wrote, "...my heart which clave unto her was torn and wounded and bleeding. And she returned to Africa, vowing unto Thee never to know any other man, leaving with me my son by her." Augustine would never go through with the marriage. Instead, he would become a priest.

Augustine had his entire life ahead of him in 373, yet he felt like he was becoming his father. His obligations toward his concubine and newborn son made him feel like he was stuck in the role of family man. For the young Augustine, it was an utterly depressing thought. He couldn't fathom the prospect of living as a slave to the demands of this world like his father had done, tied to some job and town until the day he died. He couldn't stand the thought of being like that man. Augustine had always been an introspective boy. He had always identified more with the spiritual world of Monica than the material world of Patricius. Fortunately, in 373, he read the Roman philosopher Cicero for the first time and he immediately declared himself a lover of wisdom. He had discovered philosophy, which in fact means lover of wisdom, and the introspective boy was transformed into an intellectual young man. This new world of ideas was a world away from his concubine, his newborn son, and Patricius. And so Augustine's lifelong career as an intellectual was born.

Augustine became a proud intellectual and a disciple of philosophy. The idea of rising above the crass conditions of the material world, of being lifted on a cloud of divine knowledge, appealed to his pride. But it wasn't enough. Cicero served only to whet his appetite for knowledge, so he sought wisdom in the Old Testament. And upon reading it for the first time, he declared that it was low-class compared to Cicero. To Augustine, the stories of the Old Testament seemed mired in the material world. He wanted divine knowledge, not pedestrian rules like "Thou shalt not steal." His pagan father could have told him that. To make matters worse, the particular translation he was using was written in a style of Latin that would have seemed low-class to educated Romans. So when a religious sect called the Manichees approached Augustine in 373 with the promise that he could become divine through secret knowledge, he was hooked.

The Manichees were a Christian sect from Persia, so called because they were followers of the prophet Mani. Mani lived in Babylon from about AD 216 to 276 and prospered under the reign of King Shapur I. Mani claimed to be the last prophet sent from God to mankind. He also told his followers he had received revelations from God and claimed to be the Holy Spirit. His brand of Christianity incorporated elements of Buddhism and a Persian religion called Zoroastrianism. But his unorthodox doctrines and special favor with the king made the Zoroastrian clergy despise him. They hated Mani. Indeed, as soon as he lost the king's favor and protection, they conspired to have him killed. Nobody knows exactly how Mani was put to death, but the most colorful version of the story says that he was skinned alive. Then his skin was stuffed with straw and hung at the gates of the Persian city of Gondeshapur as a warning to all.

The Manichees believed the universe was made of two kingdoms: the Kingdom of Light and the Kingdom of Darkness. God created the Kingdom of Light and it was the source of all good in the world. At the same time, the Kingdom of Darkness was the source of all evil in the world and was just as powerful as God. Together, these two kingdoms were responsible for the apparent never-ending conflict between good and evil. According to the Manichees, the battleground for this conflict was mankind. Mankind was made of the same good and evil nature as the universe, represented in man as body and soul. The soul was perfect and incorruptible, a divine part of God himself. The body, on the other hand, belonged to the Kingdom of Darkness and was constantly assailed by its evil forces.

The goal of the Manichee was to receive this knowledge as the divine revelation of man's true nature and, once revealed, identify only with the divine perfection of the soul through the sacred texts and rituals of the prophet Mani. Thus Manichaeism tried to offer something for everyone. It was Christian in that it advocated a morally perfect and ascetic life like Christ in the desert. It was Zoroastrian in that it taught the world was made of two substances, light and dark or good and evil. And it was Buddhist in that it promised release from suffering in the body through identification with the soul.

Everybody loves a secret and Augustine was no exception, especially when that secret puffed his intellectual pride. Augustine was drawn to the Manichees because they claimed to know how to break free of worldly desires and thus achieve a higher state of being. They claimed to know how to become divine like Christ. By joining the Manichees, Augustine received the secret knowledge of the supposed Kingdoms of Light and Darkness. The Manichees claimed that by receiving this esoteric knowledge, Augustine could reject the evil of his body (which meant the desire for sex and power) by choosing the perfection of his soul. And to prove it, the Manichees practiced celibacy.

Augustine the Manichee returned home to his mother's house in Thagaste in 375. After four years in Carthage, he had just finished school and had taken a job in his hometown as a teacher. His mother was shocked at what her son had become. In Monica's eyes, Augustine returned home from college with a new grandson and a concubine-in-law, and he had joined a cult. When it came to the Manichees, Monica sided with the townspeople of Thagaste. That is to say, she believed the Manichees were an illegal and heretical sect, a dangerous secret society. But Augustine, having lived and gone to school in the big city, now believed the townspeople were just a bunch of country bumpkins. Augustine, it seems, was more like his father than he cared to admit. Whereas Patricius had been proud and physical, Augustine was proud and intellectual.

When Augustine arrived at his mother's doorstep in 375, he believed he could become like God through his own intellectual power. He thought Jesus was simply an evolved Manichee, the point at which every auditor of Manichaeism must ultimately arrive. In contrast, Monica never believed she could save herself. Rather she believed she could come to God only through humility and faith in Christ. The difference between mother and son went to the heart of the Christian faith. Augustine believed he could free himself from the desire for temporal things by becoming divine like Christ. The promise of the Manichees was that of the serpent in the garden—eat of the tree of the knowledge of good and evil and ye will be as gods. On the other hand, Monica believed that release from selfish desire was possible only by receiving the free gift of God's eternal being through faith in Christ's sacrifice and his victory over death. All of which is to say that Augustine believed he could save himself, while Monica believed Jesus saves. Mother and son were indeed separated by a vast theological divide.

Monica opened her heart to her grandson, and we can imagine that she at least tolerated the mother of her grandson even if Monica never really liked the woman. But when she found out that Augustine had become a Manichee, she locked him out of the house. This went on for a while until, she believed, an angel came to her in a dream and prophesied Augustine's conversion to the Catholic faith. As if that weren't enough, she also sought the counsel of a local bishop, a former Manichee himself, who assured her that Augustine would become a Catholic. So on the word of an angel and a bishop, she let him back into the house.

A year later, Augustine returned to Carthage. He spent the next six years there, from 376 to 383, teaching at the rhetoric schools. It's not certain where his concubine and son lived during these years, but he probably left them behind at his mother's house in Thagaste. In Carthage, Augustine's career excelled. He had plenty of students and, more importantly, he was making friends in high places. The rich and powerful welcomed Augustine into their fold because of his education and superior intellect. Even back then, the rich and powerful needed to surround themselves with smart people in order to stay rich and powerful. Pretending to be smarter than the rest was one of two ways by which they justified their wealth and position to themselves and the common man. The other was by pretending to be divine or close to it. So the Roman elite were big patrons of schools, the arts, and smart men like Augustine. They were also supporters of diversions like gladiator matches and the theater to keep the rabble occupied. And if all of that failed to keep the mob in line, there was always brute force.

Augustine's star was on the rise. He was a brilliant young man in the big city who was making all the right connections. He seemed destined for greater things. But instead of finding a measure of contentment in his worldly success, he was becoming unhappier by the day. The internal conflict between his body and his soul was growing ever more intense. Soon he began to grow disenchanted with the Manichees. Some of his objections were intellectual. The Manichean story about the Kingdoms of Light and Darkness, for instance, didn't make sense. After all, everyone knew that the earth was at the center of the universe. And some of Augustine's objections to Manichaeism were theological. If God was truly God, for example, how could the Kingdom of Darkness be equal to him in power? But mostly, Augustine kept falling off the wagon by having sex. The Roman world was an inexhaustible buffet for a sex addict. From prostitutes to orgies to God-knows-what, Augustine just couldn't resist the temptation.

Augustine felt awful for failing to conquer his bodily desires. He felt awful for failing to make any progress as a Manichee. In an effort to salvage his faith, he sought the counsel of a leading Manichee, a man named Faustus of Milevum. Unfortunately for Augustine, Faustus turned out to be a self-taught man from a poor family who asked Augustine to tutor him in the liberal arts. He was more interested in gaining access to the upper class for himself and his movement than in discussing Manichean theology with Augustine. That's how a cult like the Manichees worked. Instead of standing on the merits of their doctrines, they attempted to gain influence by recruiting influential people.

At the same time, Augustine grew disenchanted with his job. He resented his students, believing they were too rowdy and unwilling to learn. He felt they didn't deserve him, that he was casting pearls before swine. By 383, Augustine felt stuck in Carthage. He was pushing thirty and had gone as far as he could with the Manichees, with his career as a teacher in Carthage, with Africa. Meanwhile, his friends who had gone on to Rome ahead of him promised Augustine better jobs, better students, and a better life across the Mediterranean. For the twenty-eight-year-old Augustine, it was time to venture into the world to seek his fortune. It was time to go to Rome.

Augustine's mother begged him not to leave. It had been eleven years since Patricius died and Monica vowed never to marry again. Augustine, her favorite son, meant the world to her. She demanded to go with him to Rome. She even followed him to the ship, which was docked at the ancient, almost mythical, colonnaded harbor at Carthage, and held onto him. But this brilliant, ambitious, and tormented young man wasn't going to be saddled with his mother in Rome. Nevertheless, what he did next was just cruel.

Augustine told his mother that he had to say goodbye to a friend at the dock. It was a lie, an attempt to give Monica the slip and sail away without her. Monica didn't take the bait. She refused to leave his side, which left Augustine feeling frustrated and angry. In order to get rid of his mother, Augustine needed a better lie. He decided to play on his mother's piety. That night Augustine convinced Monica to stay in a separate lodging so he could slip away. She agreed to it only because Augustine had arranged for her to stay in an oratory built in memory of St. Cyprian. St. Cyprian was the most revered saint in the province, and Monica was a devout Catholic. Augustine knew that his mother would trust St. Cyprian to keep her son from leaving without her. Now he wasn't just ditching his mother, he was mocking her faith. By morning Augustine was gone, leaving his mother in Africa praying and weeping.

Augustine didn't get off to a good start in the Eternal City. He wasn't long in Rome before he fell violently ill. Knowing Augustine, he was probably sick from the guilt of deserting his mother in Africa. Augustine worked as a teacher while in Rome, just as he had done in Carthage. He had hoped that the students in Rome were of a better sort than the ones in Carthage. His hopes were dashed, however, when the Roman students stiffed him on his fee at the end of the term. He would later recall how he hated these men. Apparently, students in ancient Rome paid their teachers at the end of each term. Today, colleges and universities wisely make students pay tuition at the beginning of each term.

After a miserable year in Rome, Augustine's luck began to change. Despite his waning faith in Manichaeism, membership had its privileges. The Manichees were constantly maneuvering to gain power and influence, which meant installing their own kind in influential positions whenever they could. It just so happened that in 384, the prefect of the city of Rome had been ordered by the emperor to find a new professor of rhetoric for the city of Milan. Milan was a very important city. The emperor and the Imperial Court were located in Milan, not Rome. And a professor of rhetoric was a very important post. A professor of rhetoric was responsible for delivering official public speeches, speeches which were designed to inspire the mob to revere the emperor. In an age before television news, a professor of rhetoric was charged with moving public opinion in favor of the ruling elite and their policies. Additionally, as befitting its title, the job included teaching the art of propaganda to the sons of the rich and powerful. Augustine was certainly qualified for the job, but so were a lot of other men. As is usually the case, educated men were more common than good jobs. In ancient Rome, the way to get a good, government job was to know somebody who knew somebody who had an in. Fortunately for Augustine, Catholic persecution of pagans and Manichees alike made strange bedfellows.

While in Rome, Augustine lodged in a Manichean house and had a number of Manichean friends. In turn, Augustine's Manichean friends knew the prefect of the city, a pagan named Symmachus, because they shared a common enemy—the Catholics. Symmachus was a traditional pagan from an ancient and aristocratic Roman family. He probably never imagined that the Christians would gain control of Rome. Yet by 384, Roman Catholicism had been the state religion for four years; and within that short time, Catholic persecution of pagans had reached a fevered pitch. Pagan temples had been seized and converted into churches. Pagan statues and symbols which had long adorned the public spaces of Rome had been defaced, replaced, or removed. An aristocratic pagan like Symmachus had good reason to fear and despise the Roman Catholics. Symmachus didn't care if Augustine was a pagan or a Manichee. He just wanted to make sure the job didn't go to a Catholic. So on the recommendation of his Manichean allies, Symmachus gave Augustine a perfunctory test for the position by having him recite a speech. Augustine got the job, and in the fall of 384, he moved to Milan.

Augustine was a spiritual wreck when he arrived in Milan in the fall of 384. He had never felt further from God in his life. Although he had achieved great success in his career, he had failed as a Manichee and he couldn't understand why.

Augustine would later say to a friend, "The unlearned start up and take heaven by force, and we with our learning, and without heart, we wallow in flesh and blood!" He turned again to philosophy for answers, this time to the writings of Cicero and the philosophy of the Skeptics. The Skeptics held that objective knowledge of man, God, and nature was impossible to achieve. Mankind, they believed, couldn't see the world as it was, but only as it was according to mankind's way of seeing. So when it came to philosophy, they believed it was more important to understand the questions than to know the answers. That way a man could at least hope to understand himself. Their preferred method for achieving wisdom was to suspend judgment as to whether a given proposition was true or false in favor of examining all of its possibilities. Naturally, the Skeptics laughed at anyone who claimed special knowledge of universal truths like the Manichees, which was probably why Skepticism appealed to Augustine.

Augustine flirted with Skepticism for a brief time. Having drifted from Manichaeism, he was searching for something to believe in. He was adrift at sea, so to speak. So, feeling terribly unsettled by the absence of faith, he was drawn to the idea in Skepticism of seeking to understand his questions instead of knowing their answers. But that would never be enough for Augustine. He wanted answers. In the end, Augustine never went all in with the Skeptics as he had with the Manichees. The uncertain philosophy of the Skeptics simply failed to quench his intellectual and spiritual thirst. Skepticism could neither explain why he felt and acted the way he did nor could it show him a way out.

Soon, however, Augustine met a man who preached the gospel with a certainty and understanding that seemed like it was sent from God. He met a man who showed him why he was far from God and what to do about it. There was a very good reason why Augustine had failed to reach God by his own volition. God was simply beyond his reach, and now Augustine would learn this truth from a powerful intellectual like himself. Augustine had finally met his match. He met Ambrose, the bishop of Milan.

In the fall of 384, almost four hundred years after the birth of Christ, Christians were still thinking like pagans. Most believed God had a body like a man and that mankind and God shared a single, physical universe. In other words, they believed God was a man in the sky. Augustine was still thinking like a pagan. He reasoned that if man was made in God's image, then God must be corporeal like a man. He couldn't yet fathom that his soul was made in God's image, not his body. This kind of pagan materialism had been the prevailing worldview since the dawn of civilization. The ancient Greeks, for example, believed their gods took human form and lived on Mount Olympus. It's no wonder, then, why Augustine, as a Manichee, believed he could become divine like God by his own volition. If God was merely a perfect man, then Augustine merely had to be perfect to become like God. But all of that was about to change. Ambrose, the bishop of Milan, was about to introduce Augustine to a new idea of God—God eternal.

In Milan, Augustine became a catechumen, which is a student of Catholicism preparing for baptism. However, his reasons for embracing the Catholic faith of his mother were more practical than spiritual. The Imperial Court where he worked was Christian. If Augustine wanted to do well in his new job, it helped to at least pretend to follow the same faith as his boss, the emperor. But there was another reason why he embraced the Catholic faith of his mother. His mother came to live with him in Milan. Monica, ever determined to join Augustine in Italy, made her way to Milan in the spring of 385, along with Augustine's concubine, his son, and his brother Navigius. Augustine probably figured that pretending to be Catholic was a good way to keep the peace at home. This was, after all, the same woman who had locked him out of the house in Africa for being a Manichee.

By the summer of 385, Augustine's mother, his concubine, his son, and his brother were all living under one roof in Milan. Monica, however, had never liked the concubine. So it wasn't long before she arranged a full marriage for Augustine and sent the concubine back to Africa. Her goal was to get Augustine married and baptized. Yet Augustine would have to wait because the girl Monica chose was two years too young to marry. In the end, this two-year waiting period probably saved Augustine from an unhappy marriage and an unhappy life. For within the next two years, he would experience a dramatic spiritual conversion and forego marriage in favor of the religious life. He would never marry, but he would be baptized; and that was good enough for Monica.

As a catechumen in Milan, Augustine went to church; and that's where he encountered Ambrose, the bishop of Milan. Ambrose was a celebrity with a remarkable gift for public speaking. Indeed, Ambrose was a dominant figure in Roman politics, particularly as a defender of Nicene Christianity against non-conforming beliefs. Augustine was also a practiced public speaker, and to Augustine, Ambrose's sermons were the best shows in town. He loved to attend mass just to hear Ambrose speak, which is to say he went to church mostly to be entertained. But that would change over time as the bishop's words began to resonate with Augustine.

Ambrose was an aristocrat who hailed from an ancient and noble Roman family. He was cousin to Symmachus, the prefect of Rome who had given Augustine his job as a professor of rhetoric in Milan. Ambrose had been the bishop of Milan for eleven years when Augustine began attending church there in 385. Before that, Ambrose had been the consular governor of the Liguria and Emilia regions of Italy, an appointment he had received from the emperor himself. He was among the most learned men in Milan and was fluent in Greek. This meant he could read both Greek philosophy and the New Testament in their original language. Augustine, by contrast, spoke only Latin and was forced to read Greek philosophy and the Bible in translation. Ambrose brought the full weight of his education to bear in his sermons, a feature which made them particularly appealing to the highly intellectual Augustine. Augustine was intellectual almost to the point of snobbery. But he listened to Ambrose because the bishop outranked him. Ambrose was fourteen years his senior, of a higher social class, and more highly educated than he. It took a lot to overcome Augustine's intellectual pride.

Through his sermons, Ambrose showed Augustine a side of Catholic Christianity that he had never seen before. Ambrose restored Augustine's faith in the Old Testament by showing him that the Old Testament prophets were bona fide philosophers, as erudite as any Greek or Roman, that spoke an unassailable truth. Before he met Ambrose, Augustine regarded much of the Old Testament as absurd and contrary to the teachings of Christ. The Manichees went even further. They taught that the God of the Old Testament was a devil who created the physical universe in order to cause human beings pain and suffering by trapping their souls in bodies. Ambrose resolved Augustine's conflicts with Scripture by showing him how to allegorize parts of the Old Testament, in a manner consistent with both Christianity and the accepted cosmology of the time, instead of reading them as literal fact.

But much more than this, Ambrose showed Augustine that God wasn't a man in the sky. He showed Augustine that God was a spiritual being, incorporeal and changeless, who existed outside of space and time. In other words, he showed Augustine that God was truly eternal. This was one of the most important moments in the history of Western civilization, the moment when Augustine went from thinking like a pagan to thinking like a Christian. Until this moment, Augustine understood the world like almost any pagan. He didn't necessarily believe God had a body like a man, but he did believe there was only one material universe and God was in it like any creature. Now, under the guidance of Ambrose, Augustine conceptualized heaven as an entirely separate dimension, a spiritual realm outside of space and time. Whereas Augustine had previously believed there was only one universe, now he believed there were two—the physical universe and an entirely separate spiritual universe. And in time, Augustine would build on this idea to create a new cosmology for a new Christian European civilization.

But for now, Augustine was filled with hope because Ambrose had shown him once and for all that Manichaeism was false, that the Manichees had sold him a false god that was made in man's image. He no longer felt guilty for having failed as a Manichee. Yet on the other hand, he wasn't quite ready to fully accept the God of Ambrose, a wholly spiritual God that existed outside of space and time. Augustine was angry at himself for having been hoodwinked by the Manichees. He was angry at himself for allowing the Manichees to lull him into believing doctrines that were clearly false, and which had no basis in the accepted astronomy of his time, by appealing to his intellectual pride. And he wasn't going to let it happen again.

Augustine needed to confirm that what Ambrose preached was true. Thus, in order to make the leap from the material to the spiritual, Augustine needed to find Ambrose's God in rational philosophy; and that's just what he found in the philosophy of Plato. Augustine never read anything written by Plato himself. Instead, he studied the works of the Neoplatonists, pagan philosophers like Plotinus and his student Porphyry who lived during the third century AD in Alexandria, Egypt. He first read the Platonists in June of 386. And by the end of that summer, he was a believer.

By logic and reason, the Platonists gave Augustine two things he needed in order to accept the God of Ambrose. First, they explained that the cosmos consisted of two separate universes instead of just one. They showed Augustine that there existed not only the physical universe, but a separate spiritual universe as well. And this moved Augustine to fully accept the idea that God existed outside of space of time, beyond the realm of earthly human experience. Augustine was now convinced that the separation between man and God was profound indeed, and that God was beyond the reach of men.

Second, the Platonists showed Augustine that lesser things proceeded from greater things. Just as Christians believe God created the world, so too did the Platonists believe the world proceeded from eternal ideas that existed in the spiritual universe. That is to say, they believed our physical universe of space and time proceeded from a greater spiritual realm that was eternal. And this was sufficient to convince Augustine that he could never achieve spiritual perfection by his own volition, despite what the Manichees had said. Because conversely, it meant lesser things couldn't become greater things. A dog couldn't become a man; and a man couldn't simply choose to become perfect like God. Augustine finally accepted that no man could achieve spiritual perfection without God's divine help or grace. And he finally accepted that he was powerless over his addiction to lust. Of course, unlike Christians, the Platonists believed a man could achieve spiritual perfection by turning inward to the world of ideas, which they thought connected the mind to their idea of heaven. But Augustine rejected this idea, reasoning that in this life, the soul was anchored to the earth by the body. Now, what Augustine was actually doing here was remarkable. He was using Platonism to reason away his intellectual pride and admit that he couldn't save himself. But he still had one major problem. He still didn't know how to reach God.

Augustine's searching and suffering finally came to a head in August of 386. By his own account, he was with a friend in the garden of his villa in Milan, wallowing in self-pity. He had hit bottom. Disgusted that he couldn't quit his addiction to sex and about as depressed as a man can be, he began to cry. He retreated to a corner of the garden to be alone with his grief when suddenly he heard the voice of a child say, "Take up and read. Take up and read." Augustine returned to where his friend was sitting to find a volume of St. Paul's letters which he had left there. And he found the book and he opened it and he read the first passage he opened to: "Let us walk honestly, as in the day; not in rioting or drunkenness, not in chambering and wantonness, not in strife and envying: But put ye on the Lord Jesus Christ, and make not provision for the flesh, to fulfil the lusts thereof." He had chanced upon a passage from St. Paul's Letter to the Romans. And he suddenly understood how Christ fit into the Christian-Platonic framework he had been constructing in his mind since June. He suddenly realized that he didn't go to God, but rather God came to him. He finally realized that Christ was the one mediator of God's grace, the bridge that connected man to God. Augustine's conversion was as much intellectual as it was spiritual, and it was completed when he finally figured out how all of the pieces of the Christian faith fit together. He was doing theology and he didn't even know it.

Shortly after his conversion in August of 386, Augustine quit his job in Milan and retired to a friend's villa on Lake Como to further study Platonism and grow in his new faith. In light of all he had seen, he could no longer continue as a professor of rhetoric in Milan. But he returned to Milan in March of 387 to receive baptism. And so it came to pass that St. Augustine, his son Adeodatus, and a friend were baptized by St. Ambrose, the bishop of Milan, on the night before Easter in 387.

Augustine was a new man following his baptism in 387. He had already quit his job the previous year. Now he gathered his family and some friends together and began the long trek back to Africa. As an outer sign of putting off the old man, he planned to live in Africa as a *servus Dei*, which is Latin for Servant of God. The Servants of God were baptized and celibate laymen who dedicated their lives to the Roman Catholic Church. Augustine looked forward to his new life in Africa with his friends and family. But tragically, Monica would never see Africa again.

Not long after leaving Milan, Augustine's party became stranded in Ostia by civil war. Ostia was the ancient seaport of Rome at the mouth of the Tiber River. It was vital to the life of the city, a main artery through which goods and people flowed in and out of Rome. In the fall of 387, a usurping Roman general named Magnus Maximus brought his years-long fight for the Western Empire from Gaul to Italy. Rome's emperors were constantly being challenged for the throne by usurpers. Unfortunately for Augustine, Maximus blockaded the port at Ostia in an attempt to bring the city to its knees. So Augustine and his party were forced to wait there until the naval blockade was lifted and ships were again permitted to sail for Africa.

In the meantime, they took a house. Tragically, not long after they settled into their house at Ostia, Monica fell grievously ill. She was dying; and as she lay dying, Augustine's brother Navigius bemoaned the impending tragedy of his mother's death in a foreign land. Monica wanted to be buried beside her husband Patricius at home in Africa, yet even in the face of death she remained steadfast in her faith. If her death in a foreign land was God's will, then thy will be done. She reproached Navigius, telling both of her sons not to worry about her body, but to pray for her soul. St. Monica lay dying for nine days. When she finally succumbed to the march of time, Augustine was struck with grief. He later recalled, "I closed her eyes; and there flowed withal a mighty sorrow into my heart, which was overflowing into tears; mine eyes at the same time, by the violent command of my mind, drank up their fountain wholly dry; and woe was me in such a strife!" In a single moment, the mother whom Augustine had known and loved all of his life was gone. She was fifty-six years old.

Augustine was forced to remain in Ostia for more than a year until Maximus was defeated. With his defeat, the blockade was lifted and Augustine was finally allowed to return home. He arrived in Carthage in late 388 along with his son, some friends, and his brother. After a short stay in Carthage, he returned to his hometown of Thagaste, to his father's estate, where he lived with his family and friends as a *servus Dei*. He spent most of his time contemplating philosophy and Christian doctrine, writing against the Manichees, and figuring out how to live a Christian life in this world. He was more monk than priest at this time, which is to say he was more like Christ in the desert than Christ in the city. But he was soon shaken from his ivory tower by the worst tragedy that can befall a parent. In 390, less than two years after his return home, Augustine's son Adeodatus died. The boy was only seventeen. Augustine never wrote about the death of his son. It was simply a grief too great for words. No parent ever gets over the loss of a child.

Augustine left Thagaste in 391, about a year after his son died, and traveled the road down to the port city of Hippo Regius. Today, Hippo Regius is the city of Annaba, Algeria. Augustine went to Hippo to counsel a man who was considering becoming a *servus Dei* and to find a suitable location to establish a monastery. It was while living in Hippo that Augustine was ordained a priest. He was, quite literally, drafted for the job by the local bishop.

The local bishop, an elderly Greek named Valerius, needed a priest badly and he knew few men in Hippo as qualified or as available as Augustine. As a *servus Dei*, the highly educated Augustine was almost a priest in the eyes of the bishop. So one day at mass, Valerius led his congregation to elect Augustine as their priest by having them shout forth his name and push him to the altar. There was nothing unusual about it. This form of electing priests and bishops was common at the time. Of course Augustine had second thoughts before accepting the election, and of course he went on to become an exceptional priest. His tremendous intellect and superior education made him an expert at expounding Church doctrine and refuting heresies. His talent for oratory and public debate had, in fact, made him into something of a minor celebrity. He was like the Ambrose of Hippo. The old bishop Valerius wanted to ensure that Hippo kept their prized priest, so in 395 he named Augustine as his successor. Then in 396, Valerius died and Augustine became bishop of Hippo Regius, a position he would hold until his death in 430.

Augustine was now forty-two years old. He had seen a lot in his time. His parents were gone, his son had died, he had been forced to abandon the woman he loved, and his close friends all had died or gone their separate ways. But at the same time, he had found God and had been elevated to the rank of bishop. He looked back on his life and almost couldn't believe how ignorant he had once been. Who was that boy from Thagaste all those years ago that despised his father and fell in with the Manichees? And he wanted to show the masses of people who were still thinking like pagans the wholly spiritual reality he had discovered. He wanted to free them from the world, from their desire for possessions and wealth and power and sex and domination and all manner of temporal things. So he began work on the story of his remarkable conversion to Catholicism, his *Confessions.* It was the world's first autobiography.

Augustine's *Confessions* is unlike any autobiography ever written. It is one long prayer from Augustine to God, and for that reason, it is perhaps the most intimate window into a man's soul ever made. Is there any testimony from a human being more honest or more intimate than his or her private prayer to God? Throughout the *Confessions,* Augustine stands with his back to the reader facing God while the reader overhears his prayer. But Augustine never intended his *Confessions* to be read alone. Rather, he intended his *Confessions* to be read aloud to an audience. The *Confessions* is divided into thirteen books, with each book taking about an hour to perform. So it's not really a book in the modern sense of the word, but the late Roman equivalent of television or radio. In an age when most people couldn't read, Augustine designed his *Confessions* to reach the largest audience possible. Augustine was, after all, a professional public speaker. If he could use rhetoric and oratory to move crowds to believe in the emperor, then surely he could do the same for God. Augustine's *Confessions* was first read aloud on the streets of Rome around the year 400. It introduced his life and thought to the Roman world and made him an instant celebrity. The *Confessions of St. Augustine* would in fact become the second most widely known book in the West during the Middle Ages, second only to the Bible.

Augustine spent the next decade immersed in his job as bishop of Hippo. He celebrated mass, wrote letters and treatises on Christian doctrine, counseled clergymen and laymen, combated Manichaeism and other non-conforming doctrines that had been declared heretical, and attended to the day-to-day affairs of his diocese. He probably thought his greatest challenges were behind him. But then in 410, the unthinkable happened—a foreign army marched on the city of Rome for the first time in 800 years! The empire was in shock. "If Rome can perish, what can be safe?" St. Jerome wrote from Palestine. Many Romans fled to Africa to escape the destruction, including followers of an Irish monk named Pelagius. Little did Augustine know that the fight for the soul of the West just landed at his front door.

On August 24, 410, a barbarian horde broke through the Salaria Gate and poured into the streets of Rome. The invaders were called Visigoths and Alaric was their king. For three days they pillaged the city. Those who fought back got death while those who surrendered were spared. As the barbarians poured into Rome, Roman civilization poured out. Thousands of Romans fled to Ostia where they huddled aboard ships bound for Africa and Palestine. Now under sail, they could only watch as their world disappeared beneath the horizon like the setting sun. Rome would never be home to as many people again until the twentieth century.

Alaric and his Visigoths were *foederati*, Germanic fighters who were federated with the Roman army. They were allowed to live in the empire in exchange for defending its borders against other barbarian tribes. The emperor couldn't afford to use Roman citizens to do the job. After all, who would pay the taxes needed to maintain the empire if everyone was in the army? So he used immigrants. The Romans needed the *foederati*, but they treated the immigrants like dirt and called them barbarians. Finally, when the Romans wouldn't give them citizenship or land for a home of their own, the Visigoths turned on their host.

In 410, after the emperor broke his promises and refused to make any concessions to the Visigoths, Alaric and his men sacked the Eternal City. Many Romans saw it coming and had already left Rome, including an Irish monk named Pelagius. He wisely fled Rome for the safety of Carthage in 409. Pelagius was an Irish monk who came to Rome around the year 380, and there he became a *servus Dei*. But Pelagius wasn't just another holy man. He was uncommonly brilliant, spoke fluent Latin and Greek, and he had the gift of the gab to boot. In time, he became a spiritual adviser to a large number of Roman aristocrats and their families. He was especially popular with the teenagers and the young adults. Thus it should come as no surprise that Pelagius, as spiritual adviser to the rich and famous, became a celebrity himself.

Pelagius and Augustine never met each other in Rome. During those early years, Pelagius was probably too busy making a name for himself to make time for Augustine, while Augustine was probably too self-absorbed to even notice Pelagius. They came to know each other in later years, however, by reputation. Pelagius knew Augustine as the famous bishop of Hippo who wrote the *Confessions*. Augustine, meanwhile, knew Pelagius from his writings, particularly his letters of moral exhortation that were addressed to fellow Christians. Augustine even praised these letters for being well written and to the point. There were no quarrels between the men. And things might have stayed that way if each man had stayed on his side of the Mediterranean Sea, Pelagius in Rome and Augustine in Hippo. They might have gone on believing they were part of one big, happy Roman Catholic Church; and our world might look entirely different today. But then Western civilization got lucky and Alaric sacked Rome.

When Pelagius fled Rome in 409, he berthed in Hippo before moving on to Carthage. Hippo was just up the coast from Carthage, a relatively short journey by ship. We can almost imagine Pelagius in Hippo, this Irishman from Rome meeting with local dignitaries, surrounded by an entourage of followers, many of whom hailed from some of the greatest families in the empire. He would have been quite a spectacle in fifth-century Africa. Yet the one dignitary whom Pelagius never met was Augustine, the bishop of Hippo. It seems Augustine was out of town during Pelagius' visit. The two men would, in fact, never meet during their entire lives. Pelagius stayed in Hippo for only a short time before moving on to Carthage. All in all, he stayed in Africa for about a year and then departed for Palestine. His travels in Africa likely would have gone unnoticed, too, had he not left something in Carthage that he probably should have taken with him. That something was his chief disciple, a young aristocrat named Celestius.

Celestius was a young man who came from a wealthy, aristocratic Roman family. As with many young nobles of that time, Pelagius' brand of Christianity particularly resonated with Celestius. These young aristocrats lived in a world that had one foot in Christian Europe and the other foot in the pagan Roman past. Catholic Christianity had been the official religion of the empire since only the year 380 and many Romans still clung to the pagan religion of their forefathers. It was a confusing time of morality and brutality. Men like Celestius might have grown up listening to their fathers simultaneously extol Christian piety and the classical virtue of, say, public executions.

Unsurprisingly, such a confused morality was difficult to live by for Christians and pagans alike. Pagans complained Romans were too Christian while Christians complained Romans were too pagan. One man's virtue was another man's vice. Added to this confusion was the oppressive weight of social convention to which these young men and women were bound. Their marriages were arranged, their careers were chosen for them. In contrast to all of this, Pelagius urged young men like Celestius to throw off their wealth and be like Christ.

There was nothing new or alarming about Pelagius urging his followers to renounce their wealth and take up an ascetic life. In the Bible, Christ told a rich, young man, "If thou wilt be perfect, go and sell that thou hast, and give to the poor, and thou shalt have treasure in heaven: and come and follow me." Asceticism was an ancient practice that had been taught in the West, in one form or another, since at least the Stoics. Stoicism was a school of ancient Greek philosophy that taught its followers to live in a kind of detached harmony with nature. Ascetics like the Stoics typically denied themselves physical pleasure as a way of keeping to a virtuous life. For these men and women, asceticism usually meant abstaining from sex. Sex was seen as a weakness of the flesh that tempted the spirit away from God. Augustine himself practiced a kind of asceticism after years of struggling with sex addiction. But when Celestius started debating theology in public at Carthage in 411, it began to emerge that his master had much more in mind than asceticism.

Celestius ignited a firestorm by denying the existence of original sin, which is the Christian doctrine that each person inherits the guilt of Adam and Eves' first sin. Whether one chooses to interpret the story of Adam and Eve literally, allegorically, morally, or in its anagogical or spiritual sense, its lesson about the human condition is the same. Simply put, human beings are inexorably drawn toward selfish desire because each person is born separated from God. Yet the doctrine of original sin isn't an indictment of humanity. On the contrary, it is a compassionate doctrine that opens the door to forgiveness by admitting that human beings aren't perfect. The only problem was that in the year 411, Christians in the Roman Empire didn't universally share Augustine's belief in original sin.

Celestius first attacked original sin by denying the necessity of infant baptism. Everyone agreed that adults needed to be baptized in order to wash away personal sins. But the Church was split on whether or not babies needed to be baptized because it was split on the issue of original sin. Babies haven't yet committed any sins. Therefore the only reason for baptizing them is to wash away original sin. So in saying that infants didn't need baptism, Celestius was denying the existence of original sin; and this made the African bishops furious. They had been baptizing babies for centuries and now Celestius was saying it was all for nothing. The power of baptism was one of the most awesome powers the clergy possessed. They weren't about to let some young aristocrat from Rome diminish it by denying the existence of original sin. So when Celestius applied to become a priest in 411, the African bishops saw their opportunity to condemn him for his views.

The charges against Celestius were brought by an Italian Church official who happened to be in Carthage. His name was Paulinus, and he was the deacon of the Church of Milan. Paulinus had served as secretary to Ambrose until the bishop's death in 397. And in later years, at the request of Augustine, he wrote a biography of Ambrose for which he is known today.

While in Carthage in 411, Paulinus charged Celestius with heresy and put him on trial for his views before a council of African bishops. At stake was Celestius' very future as a priest. If Celestius blew it with the bishops, then he might never have a career in the Church. Yet Celestius remained steadfast in his beliefs. He refused to recant his statements regarding original sin, arguing they were not heretical because the Bible was vague on the subject and the Church hadn't yet settled the issue. Indeed, the Church hadn't confirmed the existence of original sin yet. And even among those who accepted the idea, nobody really knew how it worked. Nevertheless, the African bishops rejected Celestius' defense. They denied his ordination to the priesthood and condemned his statements as heresy. Celestius promised to appeal his case to the pope, but he never did. Instead, he left for the Roman city of Ephesus in modern-day Turkey, where original sin wasn't such a hot issue. And there, beyond the reach of the African bishops, he was ordained a priest.

Augustine didn't learn about the trial of Celestius until after it happened. He spent most of 411 in Hippo concerned with the heresy of an African Christian sect called the Donatists. The Donatists believed the validity of a sacrament, such as baptism, depended upon the moral state of the priest who administered it. To the orthodox Catholic Church, this was like saying the efficacy of a medicine depended upon the health of the doctor who prescribed it. Augustine worked hard to defeat the Donatists because if they had prevailed, a perfect baptism would require a perfect priest; and then nobody could be sure if their baptism was valid or not. As for the trial of Celestius, Augustine first heard about it from his good friend Count Marcellinus. Marcellinus was a Roman official sent to Africa by the emperor. He was there to decide the matter of the

Donatists. Marcellinus had the legal authority to impose physical punishment for heresy against the state religion, Roman Catholicism. Roman justice usually meant flogging, beating, torture, slavery, or execution. The Romans didn't warehouse people in prisons. While living in Carthage, Marcellinus periodically sent Augustine news about the Roman refugees there. And when Augustine first heard about Celestius and the Pelagians in the winter of 411, he was appalled.

Pelagius didn't believe in original sin. Instead, he taught his followers that human beings disobeyed God's will because they had forgotten how to be good. And since men only knew evil, they were drawn to it as something desirable. The fix for mankind's condition, he taught, was the example of Jesus Christ. In his view, Christ forgave each person's individual sins by his sacrifice on the cross. Baptism, then, rendered each Christian perfect and without sin; and thereafter, it was each person's responsibility to live a perfect life by following the example of Christ. Every Christian had a duty to use his or her free will to choose the good by imitating Christ; and by choosing the good, men could achieve spiritual and moral perfection and thereby reach God.

This was the great lie in Augustine's opinion, the very lie by which the serpent in the garden deceived Eve. It was the promise that men could be as gods. The only hitch was that spiritual perfection required selflessness, and Augustine knew that human beings weren't capable of being truly selfless. No human being could liberate himself from his desire for his own well-being because to attempt to do so was an inherently selfish act. It was done either to secure a benefit or avoid a detriment, to win heaven or avoid hell. In other words, it was done in pursuit of the very thing he was trying to escape—the desire for his own well-being. Such was the case even when doing good. Men did charity to win honor; they treated others with compassion only because that was how they wished to be treated. Augustine had learned from years of suffering and searching that only God was truly selfless, and only God could liberate men from their hopeless condition through the truly selfless sacrifice of his Son, Jesus Christ.

Not surprisingly, Pelagianism appealed greatly to proud, aristocratic Romans. They were drawn to the idea that salvation was for an elite few who possessed the virtue to walk the path of moral perfection. They liked Pelagius' emphasis on free will. Pelagius even went so far as to assert that it was possible for men to lead lives completely free of sin, a statement that was sure to draw the ire of Augustine. But Pelagius wasn't a bad man. He was merely dismayed by the moral laxity that was prevalent in the late Roman Empire. He was essentially telling Romans to clean up their act and behave like better people. To that end, he told his followers that evil existed so that men could freely choose the good. So when he first heard Augustine's *Confessions* read aloud in the streets of Rome, he was repulsed by the idea that men were powerless over sin.

Augustine resolved to have Pelagianism declared heretical. This meant he would have to persuade a council of bishops to find Pelagius guilty of holding views that were contrary to Roman Catholicism. Generally, any opinion that ran contrary to Church doctrine was heresy. But neither Pelagianism nor Augustine's theology was Church doctrine. So before Augustine could so much as accuse Pelagius of heresy, he would have to establish that his own positions on original sin and grace were true. What made Pelagius a particularly formidable opponent, however, was that he had reached his conclusions by interpreting exactly the same biblical texts as Augustine, particularly St. Paul's Letter to the Romans. Never before had Augustine faced such a challenge. His fight against Pelagius would be the fight of his life, a fight that would determine nothing less than the very future of the Roman Catholic Church and Western civilization. Failure was not an option.

Augustine launched his battle against Pelagius with a writing campaign. Through a number of treatises and letters, he fully developed the tenets of Pelagianism and fleshed out his own competing doctrines of original sin and God's grace in order to show that Pelagianism was contrary to Catholic Christianity. But that was only half the battle. He still had to pin the offending doctrines on Pelagius. The problem was that the Irishman hadn't espoused his views in public like Celestius had done. There was simply no evidence tying Pelagius to Pelagianism. Then Augustine caught a break in 413 when the cantankerous St. Jerome publicly accused Pelagius of heresy.

St. Jerome is famous for giving Western civilization the Vulgate Bible, which was the first complete Latin translation of the Bible from its original Hebrew, Aramaic, and Greek. It was the Bible most commonly used in Europe until the Protestant Reformation in 1517. Jerome was a good friend of Augustine and, even more importantly, he was a famous enemy of Pelagius. The bad blood between Jerome and Pelagius went back decades, to the time when both men lived in Rome. Now, both men were living in Palestine, a land that apparently wasn't large enough for the two of them. Luckily for Augustine, Pelagius responded to Jerome's accusations the following year with a treatise entitled *On Nature*. It was the smoking gun Augustine needed to charge Pelagius with heresy, an exposition of Pelagianism from Pelagius himself.

Based on this evidence, Augustine forced Pelagius to stand trial before a council of bishops not once, but twice in the year 415. The first trial was held at Jerusalem. Officially, the charges against Pelagius were dismissed for lack of proof. But beneath the surface, the bishops in Palestine didn't want to boot a good man from the Church for what seemed like a minor disagreement over a minor issue. They just didn't think original sin was as grave a matter as Augustine's representatives made it out to be. The second trial was even more of a disaster for Augustine. It was held at Diospolis, which today is the Israeli city of Lod. There, Pelagius denied several of the charges, explained his theology in a manner that was pleasing to the bishops, and blamed the rest on Celestius. The council ended up condemning the heresy but not the heretic. In effect, Pelagius had been declared orthodox.

Augustine now had a serious problem. These councils were so prestigious that only the pope in Rome could override their rulings. In Augustine's view, desperate times required desperate measures. In 416, three hundred African bishops quickly assembled at two councils to condemn Pelagius and Celestius. One council met in Africa at Carthage, while the other met in the adjoining province of Numidia at Milevum. Each council drafted a letter to Pope Innocent I asking the pope to declare Pelagianism heretical and to excommunicate Pelagius and Celestius. Meanwhile, Augustine drafted a third letter to the pope on behalf of himself and four other bishops. These letters were then delivered to the pope along with a case file against Pelagius, which included a record of the proceedings against him and some of Augustine's writings on original sin and grace.

The pope agreed with the African bishops and excommunicated Pelagius and Celestius. Pelagius, however, was invited to appear in Rome, in person or by letter, to confirm he hadn't run afoul of Church doctrine. Pelagius chose to appear by letter, but Pope Innocent I died in 417 before he could take up the matter again. And so the fight passed to his successor Pope Zosimus. Zosimus summoned Pelagius and Celestius to Rome so that each man might confirm his faith in the Church and his obedience to its doctrine. When he was finished with his inquiry, Pope Zosimus acquitted Pelagius of heresy for lack of evidence and reserved judgment on Celestius for two months to give the African bishops an opportunity to respond. The matter seemed closed, a final defeat for Augustine and the African bishops, until someone quite unexpected intervened.

On April 30, 418, the Roman emperor Honorius, the same emperor who let Alaric and his Visigoths sack Rome eight years earlier in 410, came down on Pelagius like a hammer. It turned out that Honorius felt a bit guilty for letting the Eternal City fall to the barbarians. After all, he wasn't even in Rome when he refused to bargain with Alaric. He had been hiding in the coastal city of Ravenna because it was safer from attack. So when rioting in Rome led to a retired official being attacked by supporters of Pelagius in 418, the emperor was determined to save the Eternal City if only from itself. By Imperial decree, Honorius condemned Pelagianism as heresy and banished Pelagius and Celestius from Rome. The emperor affirmed the existence of original sin and decreed that anyone caught espousing Pelagian beliefs be brought before a civil magistrate and condemned to exile. And in condemning Pelagianism, the emperor gave Augustine's theology the force of law.

The African bishops seized on this opportunity by calling the Council of Carthage, where they passed nine canons of the

Church that codified Augustine's doctrines of original sin and grace. Finally, under heavy pressure from the African bishops and the emperor, Pope Zosimus issued his famous *Epistula tractoria* or *Encyclical Letter*, which was an encyclical that required all bishops to condemn Pelagianism and agree to the new doctrines. Augustine's theology was now Church doctrine and Roman law, while Pelagianism was a crime.

In the end, Pelagius was the grain of sand that agitated the oyster to make the pearl. As a result of Augustine's prolonged and very public battle against Pelagianism, his theology became Roman law and Church doctrine in 418. And seventy-six years later, in the year 494, Augustine's theology would provide the foundation for a new political theory which held that both kings and clergy derived their authority from the same source—the Church. In ancient Rome, the supreme authority had been the emperor. But in medieval Europe, it would be the Church. If ever there was a moment that marked the end of the Roman world and the beginning of the Middle Ages, this was it. In Western Europe, the Roman Catholic Church was the most prominent institution to survive the collapse of the Western Roman Empire in 476. And as pagans throughout Western Europe converted to Catholic Christianity, a new medieval European civilization, united in faith and politics and culture, would take shape around the Church like an ecosystem taking shape around a coral reef.

The new political theory came to be known as the doctrine of the Two Powers. Ever since Emperor Theodosius I made Christianity the official religion of the Roman Empire in 380, tensions between emperors and popes mounted over a lingering question: who was the head of the Church, the emperor or the pope? Finally in 494, Pope Gelasius I put to rest any doubt that the clergy ran the Church in a letter called *Duo sunt*, which is known in English as the *Two Powers* or *Two Swords*. And the doctrine of the Two Powers that emerged from it became the basis for the authority of emperors and kings in Europe throughout the Middle Ages.

In addressing a controversy between the Holy See and the Eastern Roman emperor in Constantinople, the pope wrote, "There are two powers, august Emperor, by which the world is chiefly ruled, namely, the sacred authority of the priests and the royal power. Of these that of the priests is the more weighty, since they have to render an account for even the kings of men in the divine judgment." In accordance with Augustine's theology, the pope conceded the worldly power to the emperor, which was the power to rule over men's bodies in order to maintain the law and protect people from themselves. Yet at the same time, the pope reserved a far greater power exclusively for the clergy, which was the power to save men's souls. This meant that the priests had the exclusive power to mediate God's grace *in persona Christi* or in the person of Christ; and that conversely, the Church had the power to excommunicate any person from communion with God, including the emperor. But what did Augustine say that allowed Pope Gelasius to make such an audacious claim?

In the course of battling Pelagius, Augustine had used philosophy and Scripture to prove that Christ was the bridge that connected man to God; and that the Church was the only institution on earth that connected man to Christ. So in order to be in communion with Christ, a person had to be in communion with his Church. In Augustine's theology, this idea was merely one of many. Indeed, Augustine constructed a grand cathedral of doctrine more glorious than the most resplendent cathedral of glass and stone. He developed doctrines that are shared today by Catholics, Protestants, and Eastern Orthodox Christians alike, including the doctrines of original sin and God's grace. But this idea was the one upon which the doctrine of the Two Powers most directly relied. Thus, building upon Augustine's doctrine that explained how the Church was, as the apostle Paul wrote, the Body of Christ, Pope Gelasius asserted his authority as the successor of Peter to remind the emperor that the clergy stood in the place of Christ on earth, not the monarch. And in so doing, the pope articulated a new theory of government that would serve as the foundation for the authority of monarchs and the superior authority of the Church in Western Europe for the next thousand years; namely, that the divine right of monarchs to rule over their subjects flowed from the Church as the living Body of Christ on earth.

But there was something else. There was something in Augustine's theology that would one day make our modern world possible. Augustine's doctrines, as well as the political ideas that flowed from them, were based on the cosmology that he had learned from Ambrose and the Platonists. By adopting Augustine's theology, Western Europe adopted a new cosmology and jettisoned the old pagan Roman way of looking at the universe.

Before Augustine, most people saw the cosmos as one material universe. After Augustine, they would begin to see the cosmos as two universes: the physical universe and a wholly spiritual realm that Augustine called the highest heaven. He called it the highest heaven because the ancients called outer space the heavens. According to Aristotle and the Roman astronomer Ptolemy, the earth sat at the center of the universe while the sun, moon, stars, and planets revolved around the earth in orbits called heavens. The last heaven, or the heaven of God, was called the highest heaven. But Augustine's highest heaven was unique. In fact, it was a giant leap forward for mankind.

Augustine's highest heaven was the one thing that Plato and Aristotle said couldn't exist—it was an infinite space or a void. Through his theology, Augustine revealed a heaven that was an infinite space and thereby made the concept of infinite space real to the Christian mind. And this space, combined with certain concepts from the Christian faith, would one day give rise to our modern world.

How he did it is a bit technical. When Augustine borrowed Plato's model of the cosmos to explain Christianity, he made some changes. Plato believed the spiritual universe created the physical universe through a chain of causes or intermediary intelligences. Basically, one idea created the next idea in an unbroken chain. Plato called his heaven the realm of ideas and thought the first idea was the eternal idea of the good, which is a concept Christians might associate with God. So working from this model, Augustine eliminated all of those ideas because according to the Bible, the Judeo-Christian God created the universe and everything in it *ex nihilo* or out of nothing. In philosophical language, Augustine eliminated the intermediary intelligences from the Neoplatonic model of the spiritual universe because the Judeo-Christian God created and continually creates the universe and everything in it *ex nihilo* or out of nothing. This was how the concept of infinite space or a void became real to the Christian mind.

In the centuries to follow, the Christian West would rise above the physical universe in this space to observe man and nature with the divine detachment of Augustine's transcendent God. And man would use this power to make models of the natural world in laboratories and unlock its secrets. And he would come to see himself as an individual against the background of this space to proclaim, "We hold these truths to be self-evident, that all men are created equal, that they are endowed by their Creator with certain unalienable Rights, that among these are Life, Liberty and the pursuit of Happiness." But all of that was yet to come. Before the Christian West could make its unprecedented leaps in science, technology, and government, the Western mind would have to make an equally remarkable leap into Augustine's highest heaven—a phenomenon which would begin to occur in little more than a century in Christian Ireland.

Augustine died in Hippo Regius on August 28, 430, at the age of seventy-five. As he lay dying, Augustine found his city besieged by a barbarian tribe called the Vandals. They came to North Africa to loot the empire of all its treasure. They didn't realize Rome had risen to greatness on its ideals, not its possessions. They didn't realize that Augustine had harnessed the selfish desires of men for a new purpose—to liberate men from themselves. As for Pelagius, little is known of what happened to him after he was banished from Rome. Some say he traveled to Palestine, eventually settling in Egypt. Still others hold that he returned to Ireland. Wherever he may have gone, the future for Pelagianism seemed dark. Meanwhile, at the westernmost edge of Europe, on an island that had never known Roman rule, something extraordinary was about to happen. The Roman Catholic Church was about to launch an unprecedented mission to a land beyond the farthest reaches of the empire. The new theology was about to meet a civilization that was completely alien from the one that gave birth to it. There was no telling how the Christian faith might be affected by its new host. Augustine was coming to Ireland and the world would never be the same again.

CHAPTER TWO

A Slave in Ireland Sows
the Seed of a New Civilization

ugustine hadn't been dead a year before his ideas were on their way to pagan Ireland. In 431, seemingly out of nowhere, the Roman Catholic Church launched a mission to convert the Irish to Christianity. To the average Roman, trying to make Roman Catholics out of Irish pagans seemed like madness. But there was method to this madness. Rome's mission to Ireland was the answer to a serious problem, and that problem was the emperor.

For some time now, Roman emperors were of the opinion that they exercised final authority over the Church instead of the pope. After all, the Roman Catholic Church was the state church and the Roman emperor was the head of state. In the emperor's mind, he gave the Church its earthly authority by putting the full might and power of the Roman Empire behind it. It wasn't that the emperor wanted the pope's job as supreme pastor of the Catholic Church. It was simply that whenever religion crossed into politics or touched on the civil power, the emperor called the shots.

The pope got the message loud and clear when Emperor Honorius settled the score between Augustine and Pelagius in

418. Emperor Honorius set a troubling precedent by condemning Pelagius and giving Augustine's doctrines of original sin and grace, along with his cosmology, the force of law. Honorius had effectively forced the papacy to make Augustine's theology Catholic doctrine, and now the emperor's authority over the Church knew no bounds. Naturally, the pope felt as though he had been demoted from head of the Roman Catholic Church to just another Imperial official.

Honorius died in 423 and was succeeded by a new emperor, but it was too late. The damage had been done. The papacy needed to get out from under the thumb of the emperor, but how? How do you tell the head of state that he doesn't rule the state church? The solution was obvious. The Church needed to establish itself as an institution that was larger than the state. Whereas the emperor's jurisdiction was limited to the borders of the Roman Empire, the Church needed to show that its power to save men's souls extended to the entire world. The Catholic Church needed to show the emperor that it was truly a universal church. And to do that, it needed to do something that it hadn't done before. The Church needed to establish itself in a land that was outside of the Roman Empire. This, too, was complicated by the fact that the Roman Empire occupied most of the known world. So when the bishops rolled out the map to decide where to go, the only land that fit the bill was an island to the west of Britain that the Romans called *Hibernia*. The people who lived there named the land *Éirinn* for their pagan goddess Ériu. Today, we call it Ireland.

Rome's mission to Ireland in 431 was an extraordinary venture. Never before had the Roman Catholic Church launched a mission to preach the gospel beyond the borders of the Roman Empire. The apostle Paul had brought the gospel to the gentiles in the first century AD. And Christians working individually in the service of their faith had converted the Kingdoms of Armenia and Ethiopia in the fourth century, before the time of Augustine. But the institution of the Roman Catholic Church had never launched an official mission to convert a foreign people to Christianity, and particularly to Augustine's Catholicism. Moreover, no one in Rome fully considered how the Irish might adapt the faith to their civilization.

Rome sent Ireland her first bishop in the year 431. His name was Palladius and his mission was to convert not just some of the Irish, but the entire island. The Church couldn't trump the emperor by winning over merely a handful of converts. It needed to lay claim to an entire people. But, of course, the pope couldn't tell the emperor that he was sending a mission to Ireland to show the world who really ruled the Church. The pope needed an excuse, a reason to go to Ireland that made the mission seem like it was in the best interest of the empire.

Fortunately for the papacy, Augustine had done such a good job of purging the empire of Pelagians that, by 430, they had been pushed all the way to Britain. The Church had already sent a mission to Britain in 429 to combat the Pelagians. Now, in 431, it would launch a mission to Ireland under the pretext of routing Pelagianism before it spread there too. Granted, the men who actually went to Ireland truly believed they were there for the sole purpose of saving men's souls by converting them to Augustine's Catholicism. The pope in Rome, however, knew better.

When Palladius landed on the south coast of Ireland in the year 431, a handful of Christians had already been living there for quite some time. This small, unorganized community of believers was the product of many years of trade between Roman Britain and Ireland, particularly the slave trade. Many of the slaves traded to the pagan Irish were, in fact, Christians; which is to say the first Christians in Ireland were, in fact, slaves. But now Palladius, and at least three more bishops after him named Auxilius, Iserninus, and Secundinus, endeavored to bring the full presence of the Roman Catholic Church to the island. They set about building churches in the south of Ireland, ministering to the Christians who were already there, and converting anyone they could. Yet more than ten years into it, Rome's goal of converting the Irish on a grand scale remained elusive. If the goal of their mission was to convert the entire island, then their mission was a failure. The bishops sent by Rome never pushed beyond southern Ireland. They simply couldn't overcome the barriers of language and culture to make Catholics out of Irishmen. If the Church was ever going to convert Ireland to Christianity, then it needed a different sort of man. It needed a man who understood the Irish and the Romans, a man with one foot in the Roman Empire and the other foot in ancient Ireland. It needed a man like St. Patrick.

St. Patrick was born to an aristocratic, landowning family in Roman Britain around the time Augustine and Pelagius were locked in their titanic battle of ideas. Patrick wrote that he lived in the town of Bannaventa Berniae, but the exact location of the town is unknown. Patrick's Latin name was Patricius, a name that meant noble or well-born. Patrick didn't write very much about his parents or his childhood. His father was Calpornius and his mother was Concessa. Like Augustine's father, Patrick's father was a decurion. His job included the duties of city councilor and tax collector; and in the great Roman tradition of nepotism, Patrick probably expected to inherit his father's government job one day. Yet even more telling of the times was the fact that both Patrick's father and his grandfather were clergymen. The rule of clerical celibacy in the Catholic Church wasn't strictly enforced until the eleventh century. So Patrick's grandfather, Potitus, was a Catholic priest and Patrick's father was a deacon—and for good reason. The staggering cost of maintaining the Roman Empire was exacted from its citizens in the form of crushingly high taxes. Clergymen, however, didn't have to pay taxes.

Every saint has a past and Patrick was no exception. By his own admission, he had turned his back on God despite the fact that both his father and grandfather were clergymen. He was the typical preacher's son, so to speak. In the tradition of the Roman aristocracy, he was expected to attend school. But beyond that, it's likely he was idle. The real work of running the household and working the fields was done by servants and slaves. Patrick was raised from an early age to believe he was superior among men. He acted as he pleased and treated people like possessions.

Patrick's upbringing as a master among slaves culminated in a terrible sin when he was about fifteen years old. It was an act so terrible that it would haunt him for the rest of his life, even calling into question his fitness as bishop of Ireland some thirty years later. Early in his career as a priest, Patrick confessed his sin. And thirty years later, the priest who heard his confession divulged it to Patrick's fellow bishops. Worse yet, the priest was also Patrick's close friend. We don't know why Patrick was betrayed as an adult nor do we know what Patrick did as a teenager that was so terrible. Patrick never disclosed what he had done in any of his writings. He didn't need to because the bishops already knew exactly what he had done. He wrote only that it was something he had done in the space of an hour. Murder, idolatry, and fornication were the only sins grave enough to bring Patrick's fitness as a bishop into question. Whatever he may have done, Patrick was an arrogant lout whose time had come. His life of comfort and privilege was about to vanish like the wind.

Patrick's life changed forever one fateful night when a pagan Irish war band raided his family's villa and carried him off into the darkness, to Ireland where the young master was made a slave. "I was then nearly sixteen years old," Patrick wrote. Slave raids by the Irish were common in western Britain throughout the fourth and fifth centuries. Small bands of Irish warriors called *fianna* would often quietly slip ashore looking for Roman treasure and anyone they could take as a slave, particularly women. In pagan Irish society, the *fianna* were recognized families of brothers-in-arms. Later, they came to be despised in Christian Ireland for their pagan beliefs and violent ways. On the night they came for Patrick, they would have moved by stealth toward the villa and waited until just the right moment to attack. The sight of Roman soldiers would have almost certainly scared them off. Using lightning-fast speed and the element of surprise, they stormed the villa, killing anyone who opposed them and taking treasure and women and a boy named Patrick. Then, almost as quickly as they came, they made their retreat. Of all the members of Patrick's family, only Patrick appears to have been captured. His parents must have gone unharmed or they weren't at the villa when the raid occurred because Patrick mentions them later in his writings. Patrick was probably tied to the other slaves and marched hurriedly to a small boat waiting at the coast. One moment Patrick was a master, the next he was a prisoner; and soon he would be a slave in a foreign land. The *fianna* counted on speed and confusion for the successful raid of a Roman settlement. By the time Patrick realized what had happened to him, he might have already been halfway to Ireland.

Patrick's Roman citizenship and aristocratic pedigree afforded him no special treatment among the Irish. He was just one more British slave among many on the island. In pagan Ireland, the slave class included criminals, slaves by birth, prisoners of war, and kidnap victims like Patrick. Slaves from overseas like Patrick were more highly prized than natives because they couldn't as easily escape. Patrick spoke British as his native language, which was a language closely related to Welsh. But he probably also spoke Latin and some Irish, which he could have learned from his father's slaves. The Romans in Britain kept a good number of Irish slaves, which they acquired by force and through trade with the Irish.

Patrick would spend his entire time in bondage on a farm in northwest Ireland where he was made to tend sheep. An Irish farm more closely resembled something from the Iron Age than anything from the Roman world. Patrick's farm was probably a small tract of land, enclosed by a circular stone or earthen wall, with stone or sod huts for the people and open pens for the animals. Life on the farm was hard. As a shepherd, Patrick often slept outside with his flocks. He likely endured bad food, bad weather, and bad treatment at the hands of his master.

Yet Patrick's greatest source of suffering probably wasn't anything physical. His enslavement in Ireland had stripped him of everything, including his very identity. Not only was he likely to never again see his family and friends, but he would never be that member of the Roman aristocracy whom he had been since birth. Patricius was dead. He would later write, "... and the Lord brought on us 'the anger of his fury,' and scattered us among many nations, even to the uttermost parts of the earth, where now obscurity seems to be my lot, amongst a foreign people." Patrick was Jonah and Ireland was the belly of the fish. And Patrick was in the belly of the fish six long years.

On that lonely hillside in the northwest of Ireland, Patrick experienced a conversion to the Christian faith. Sixteen-year-old Patrick wasn't a believer even though he had been raised as a Christian. Yet by his own account, he prayed constantly in Ireland, probably because prayer was his only source of comfort. And through many years of prayer on that lonely hillside, Patrick came to believe that God had cast him into bondage for a purpose. He came to believe that God had made him a slave in order to open his eyes to his sinfulness. Patrick never expounded on this point. But we can reasonably surmise that in Ireland, he experienced how it felt to be stripped of his humanity and treated like an object; and for the first time, he saw that it was wrong. For the first time in his life, he was ashamed and sorry for how he had treated others like objects back in Britain. He was disgusted with himself and he wanted to change, so Patrick surrendered to Christ and put his trust in God. Christ was the good shepherd and Patrick was his lost sheep. And Patrick came to believe that God's plan all along was for the good shepherd to rescue his lost sheep. Hence he was no longer Patricius, but the man who would become a saint.

After six years as a slave on an Irish farm, one night Patrick heard a voice say to him, "Thou dost well to fast, and shalt soon return to thy country." And again, just a short time later, he heard the voice say, "Behold, thy ship is ready." Patrick waited for a little while and then ran away, and he kept going for 200 miles! Patrick probably meant 200 Roman miles, which would be equal to about 185 of our miles. Even so, it was a tremendous distance to traverse on foot. Nobody knows the details of Patrick's flight to freedom through the Irish countryside or even how long it took. Patrick's trek through the interior of the island was almost certainly difficult and, above all, wet. As every Irishman well knows, Ireland is shaped like a bowl. High cliffs and mountains form a ring around the island, sloping down into a saturated interior of rivers and bogs. Cold and wet and miserable, Patrick knew he would be put to death if caught. One can imagine Patrick running for his life like an escaped prisoner in an old Hollywood movie, the specter of death chasing him like a pack of barking dogs.

Eventually, Patrick came to a harbor where he saw several men launching a boat for Britain. He tried to buy passage across the sea, but the men refused. "Don't at all think to go with us!" the skipper said. Then the men suddenly had a change of heart and Patrick was welcomed as one of the crew. Patrick later wrote, "But, for fear of God, I would not suck their nipples." Evidently, sucking another man's nipple was the ancient Irish equivalent of burying the hatchet. But Patrick would not submit to their pagan customs. No matter, Patrick's refusal to suck their nipples was no impediment to joining the crew. Soon he was on his way home to Britain.

The journey across the Irish Sea to Britain took three days. Then he spent another twenty-eight days trekking through Britain. He wrote, "...for twenty-eight days we journeyed through a desert." Some of this is almost certainly metaphorical, meant to convey Patrick's spiritual journey "through a desert" from captivity to freedom. But much of it is also factual, like when his party ran out of food and began to starve. Their leader turned mockingly to Patrick, like the bad thief who was crucified alongside Christ, and told him to pray to his Christian God for deliverance from their impending deaths from starvation. Patrick didn't miss a beat.

"Turn faithfully and with your whole heart to the Lord our God," Patrick replied, "—for to him nothing is impossible—that he may send food into your path today, even until you are satiated, for it abounds everywhere to him."

Suddenly, a herd of pigs appeared before them, which was the favorite food of the Irish. The men wasted no time in killing the pigs, and for two nights they gorged on swine. Even their dogs ate until they were full. Now the men respected Patrick and his God, offering him a share of some wild honey that they had found. But Patrick refused their gift when he learned they intended it as a sacrifice to their pagan gods.

Later that night, Patrick had a peculiar and terrifying encounter. "But the same night, while I was asleep, Satan, of whom I will be mindful as long as I shall be in this body, tempted me strongly, and fell on me like a great rock, so that I was unable to move my limbs." At sunrise, Patrick cried out to Elias for deliverance from evil, a cry he believed was actually the spirit of Christ crying through him; and again he was able to move his body.

Patrick ended the story of his escape by writing that his party traveled for ten more days with plenty of food and good weather until, finally, he was home in Bannaventa Berniae. Patrick wasn't an especially talented writer, but he had a great story to tell. Six years earlier, his parents had given him up for dead and now he had returned home a changed man. We can only imagine the looks on his parents' faces when Patrick walked through the door.

After six years of slavery in Ireland, twenty-one-year-old Patrick returned home to Bannaventa Berniae like a soldier returning home from war. The town probably looked the same, but he had changed. Patrick's parents could hardly have expected him to just pick up where he left off. "[They] besought me earnestly that then at least, after so great tribulations as I had endured, I should not go away from them any more," Patrick wrote. With his education cut short by his enslavement in Ireland, Patrick would have been far behind his peers. This deficit in his education was something that would bother Patrick for the rest of his life, particularly at times when writing proper Latin was required to correspond with his fellow bishops. Regardless of the gap in Patrick's education, he still stood to inherit his father's position as decurion. But after having been a slave for six years, and after his extraordinary spiritual transformation in Ireland, could he ever go back to being a master of slaves? The answer to that question for Patrick came in the form of a series of visions.

In Patrick's first vision, a man from Ireland named Victoricius gave him a letter that read, "The Voice of the people of Ireland. We entreat thee, holy youth, to come and walk still among us." Patrick believed the Irish were begging him to return with the gospel. Then he had a second vision in which he heard a voice speaking within his soul. He wondered to whom the voice belonged until he heard the words, "Who for thee laid down his life?" Now it wasn't just the Irish who were speaking to Patrick in his dreams, but Christ was too! Patrick's last vision was perhaps the most dramatic of the three. He felt some kind of divine presence within him praying. Then the divine presence seemed to hover above what Patrick called his "inner man." Patrick wrote, "...but at the end of the prayer he declared that it was The Spirit." Patrick needed no further convincing. He knew now that God had called him to bring the gospel to Ireland.

Patrick might have been champing at the bit to get back to Ireland, but his parents almost certainly disapproved. Of everything they could have wanted for their son, the last thing they wanted was for Patrick to return to Ireland. Fortunately for Calpornius and Concessa, Patrick couldn't just go to Ireland and start preaching. Patrick first needed to be ordained a priest after a long and rigorous course of study. They probably hoped their son's lengthy religious training would provide sufficient time for him to cast off any crazy ideas about preaching the gospel to barbarians. And then there were the benefits of being a priest like not having to pay taxes. In the late Roman Empire, Catholic clergy enjoyed special tax exemptions. Patrick's father knew well the financial benefits of being a deacon in the Church.

Nobody knows what Patrick did in between the time he announced his intention to return to Ireland and the time when he actually began his mission there. But it's a good guess he spent these years studying to become a priest. Legend has it that Patrick studied for the priesthood in the monasteries of Gaul. While a trip to Gaul was possible, Patrick could also have received his training closer to home in Britain. The key fact here is that he trained in the monasteries of Western Europe, which by that time had been heavily influenced by certain beliefs and practices from the Church in Egypt. Patrick would bring to Ireland not only the Roman Catholicism of Augustine, but Egyptian monasticism as well. Patrick was the bridge that linked Ireland to fifth-century Rome and the monasteries of the Egyptian desert. Later, this would prove to be far more consequential than anyone at the time had realized.

With his religious training complete, Patrick was ready to return to Ireland as a missionary. The popular account of Patrick's life says he landed in Ireland as a missionary in 432 following the death of Bishop Palladius in 431. But that account is probably more fiction than fact, a story told centuries later by Patrick's boosters to portray him as the unrivaled apostle to the Irish. More accurately, Patrick began his mission in Ireland perhaps as much as a generation after Palladius first landed there in 431. He owed a lot to Palladius and his successors. Patrick's dream of preaching the gospel in Ireland surely would have died on the vine had there not already been an official Church mission to accommodate it. But whereas the bishops from the continent never made it beyond southern Ireland, Patrick would succeed at bringing Christianity to the entire island. Indeed, millions of people around the world celebrate St. Patrick's Day every March 17 to honor his achievement. Yet that's only part of the story. There was something else, something about Patrick's Christianity that was different from what Palladius and the other bishops had brought to Ireland years before. There was something embedded in Patrick's Christianity that would, in time, unlock the door to Augustine's highest heaven. But before that could happen, Patrick first had to win the hearts and minds of the people. He had to make Christians out of Irishmen. And as it turned out, he was uniquely qualified for the job.

Patrick had an advantage over Palladius and the other bishops who had previously been sent by Rome—he had already lived in Ireland for six years as a slave before beginning his mission there. Patrick spoke the Irish language, had a working knowledge of Ireland's customs and laws, and knew how to get permission from local kings to travel freely throughout their kingdoms. The problem of traveling in ancient Ireland cannot be overstated. The decentralized, tribal structure of ancient Irish society made travel on the island far more difficult than in the Roman Empire. Travel in the Roman Empire was facilitated by documents from perhaps only one official who ultimately answered to the emperor. By contrast, ancient Ireland had hundreds of minor kings from whom Patrick needed permission in order to travel in their kingdoms. As a result, Patrick had to continually give gifts to the various kings or their judges, or he had to travel with the sons of kings, in order to move freely about the island. Patrick's gift giving required him to raise money from his followers, a practice which eventually led to accusations of graft by his fellow bishops in Britain. Later he would be forced to answer these charges.

As Patrick traveled throughout Ireland, he attracted converts from all ranks of society. He ministered to royalty, but was more successful at converting the children of kings than the kings themselves. Winning over kings or future kings was vitally important to Patrick's success. Once Patrick had won over a king, his subjects shortly followed. Patrick also ministered to those who had no power like women and slaves. Patrick's call to the celibate life seems to have been exceptionally popular among Irish women, perhaps because it gave them some dominion over their own bodies instead of being the property of a man. Slaves, on the other hand, had no control over their bodies. Nonetheless, they likely identified with Christ's suffering and took comfort in the promise of a better life to come. Patrick was in fact one of the first people in recorded history to condemn slavery, particularly the enslavement of Christians. When a Christian warlord in Britain named Coroticus murdered and enslaved a number of Patrick's converts, Patrick wrote a letter condemning him and his soldiers on the grounds that it was in violation of Scripture for Christians to murder and enslave fellow Christians. Patrick argued for a kind of basic equality among Christians when he wrote, "Are we not from one stock, and have we not one God for our Father?" Interfaith marriage was probably another way by which Patrick won new converts. In these marriages, usually the wife was the Christian spouse. It should come as no surprise that the greatest influence on a man's spiritual life is often his wife. Once Patrick had won over the wives, the husbands shortly followed.

The greatest opposition to Patrick's mission was to be expected from the druids, who were the pagan priests of ancient Ireland. They had the most power and influence to lose from pagans converting to the new religion. Surprisingly, the druids seem to have been relatively tolerant of Christianity; and it may have been their tolerance which led to their demise. In paganism, there was almost always room for one more god.

Christianity, on the other hand, is understandably intolerant of other gods. In Christianity, there is only one true God and missionaries like Patrick would have forced people to choose between deities. Along with this choice, there came the threat of eternal damnation in hell for not worshipping the Christian God. Surely, some pagans would have converted to Christianity for this reason alone.

Although there were many reasons why a pagan in ancient Ireland might convert to Christianity, the one most over-looked is the strength of the Christian message itself. Like most pagans, the ancient Irish lived in a universe that was caught in an endless life and death cycle: crops were planted only to be harvested; livestock was killed so that people could eat; old people died so that children could be born. Time and space were represented as a circle, marked by the rising and setting of the sun. This was the cosmic round. The Irish constructed their pagan religion around this idea and they believed in rein-carnation. But there was a catch. The gods continued to give crops and livestock and children only so long as they received something in return. The currency of this life and death cycle was sacrifice, including animals and even human beings. The pagan gods were as selfish as the human beings who created them. But like a mighty thunderclap, Patrick came into this world preaching a story of a single Creator who sacrificed his Son for them. It was a revolution. Jesus Christ was the sacrifice to end all sacrifices because through his death and resurrection, he brought eternal life and ended the life and death cycle of the pagan gods. And the most amazing thing of all was that not one human or animal sacrifice was required in order to receive this boon. The currency of the new religion was faith, not animal and human sacrifice. As the New Testament says, "For

God so loved the world, that he gave his only begotten Son, that whosoever believeth in him should not perish, but have everlasting life." For a people who were accustomed to always making sacrifices to appease their selfish gods, Christianity offered a new deal.

Patrick's success at evangelizing the Irish was truly remarkable. He brought the Irish to the Christian faith by his love of God. His mission saw the conversion of nearly all the Irish to Christianity without bloodshed, without fighting. The light of his faith made others want to believe. Indeed, Patrick was so successful at evangelizing the Irish that within a generation after his death, Irish paganism was already headed for the ashbin of history. Eventually, Patrick was made bishop of Ireland. His fitness as bishop, however, was called into question some years later when his confessor divulged that grave sin he had committed when he was fifteen years old. His fellow bishops in Britain used the occasion to further accuse him of keeping Church monies that he had raised from his converts. It was mostly sour grapes. Some of the bishops were jealous that Patrick, a man who wasn't politically connected within the Church, took a job that nobody wanted and made it into a very important position. They were jealous of his success. Patrick responded to the charges by writing his *Confession*, which was a letter addressed to his fellow bishops in Britain detailing the events of his life, his captivity in Ireland, his spiritual transformation as a slave, his love for the Church, and his love for the Irish. It survives to this day and is an invaluable source for the events of his life. And most importantly, it persuaded the

Church to allow him to remain as bishop of Ireland for the remainder of his years.

Nobody knows exactly when Patrick died, only that he died near the end of the fifth century. By then the Roman Empire had fallen and a new Christian Europe was emerging from the ashes of that once great civilization. When he died, Patrick was already being called a saint for evangelizing the Irish. But that's only part of the reason why Patrick is so important. Equally important was the kind of Christianity he brought to Ireland.

When Rome first sent Palladius to Ireland in 431, it intended to make the Irish Church in its image. This meant organizing Irish churches into territorial units. In the Roman Empire, the Roman Catholic Church was organized into territories called dioceses. This system was based on the old Roman system of governing towns by grouping them into territorial districts under the rule of a single governor. Accordingly, each Church diocese was comprised of several towns in a given territory; and all of the churches and clergy within those towns were governed by a bishop. As the place where the average Roman came to worship and to learn about his faith, the diocesan church was the primary vehicle for communicating the Christian faith to the people of the empire.

The situation in Ireland, however, was strikingly different. Thanks to Patrick and his followers, monasteries became the primary vehicle for communicating the faith in Ireland. Patrick sowed the seed of monasticism in Ireland, constantly winning converts to the monastic life. For him, the ascetic life was the greatest way for a man or a woman to serve God in this life, either as a monk or a nun. Astonishingly, for a way of life that originated as far away as Egypt, the Irish took to the

monastic life like ducks to water. The growth of Irish monasticism was so explosive in the decades after Patrick's death
that by the years 535-540, the first full-fledged monasteries
appeared on the island; and by the middle of the sixth century,
the monastery was well on its way to becoming the dominant
religious institution in Ireland.

In contrast to diocesan churches, monasteries were independent of episcopal control. This meant they didn't answer
to the local bishop. They were founded as communities of
monks or houses; and each house was governed by an abbot
who was chosen by his monks. Remarkably, within a century after Patrick had died, these abbots were running the
Irish churches. Of course there were still bishops in Ireland
to carry out certain religious and ceremonial functions. But
the responsibility of governing churches now fell to the abbot
instead of the bishop. This was very different from how things
were done on the continent.

But the thing that really set the monasteries apart from
diocesan churches was penance. Diocesan churches offered
only public penance, which was a kind of one-time second
baptism for the forgiveness of murder, idolatry, or fornication. Today, Christians of the many denominations take it for
granted that they can ask God for forgiveness or go to confession. But for the average Christian living in the Roman
Empire, there was no repeatable mechanism for the forgiveness
of sin. The monks, however, were the exception to the rule.
They repeatedly confessed their sins and did penance within
the monastery to obtain forgiveness for any sin at any time.
Quite simply, the monks had a repeatable mechanism for the
forgiveness of sin while the bishops and priests in the diocesan
churches did not.

Because Patrick received his clerical training at the monasteries in Western Europe, he brought all of this with him to Ireland. And within a century following Patrick's death, the monks of Ireland would do two extraordinary things with his legacy. First, they would combine traditional Irish learning with monasticism to create monastic schools. Education had always been a sacred function in pagan Irish society and now, in early Christian Ireland, it would become a function of the monasteries. And these monastic schools would go on to become the main repositories of Greek and Latin learning in Western Europe during the Early Middle Ages.

Second, and even more important than the schools, the Irish monks would combine the monastic practice of penance with Irish law and custom to develop something entirely new and revolutionary. They would develop a repeatable mechanism for the forgiveness of any sin at any time for anyone in Ireland, not just for the monks in the monasteries. They were about to radically change the way Christians in the West experienced their faith by bringing confession and penance out of the monastery to every Christian in Ireland and beyond. They were about to make penance a fully integrated part of Augustine's Catholicism. And in so doing, they would utterly transform Western civilization.

CHAPTER THREE

The Secret Gospel of Ireland

*A*t *the dawn* of the fifth century, a man fled the Egyptian desert with something so powerful that it would change the West in untold ways. His name was John Cassian. John was a very spiritual man who dwelt for many years among the monasteries of Egypt searching for God. According to legend, John was so spiritual that he repudiated the flesh by castrating himself. So when a controversy arose as to whether God had a physical body or was a purely spiritual being, John held with those who favored the spirit. The bishop of Alexandria, on the other hand, held with those who favored the body; and those who opposed the bishop faced the very bodily threat of persecution, so John fled Egypt. Yet persecution would prove to be providential. For John carried something out of the Egyptian desert—from Alexandria to Constantinople to Rome and finally to Marseilles—which, in the hands of the Irish monks, would radically change the way Christians in Western Europe experienced their faith.

John Cassian was born around the year 360 in a part of the Roman Empire that is now Romania. When he was a young man, perhaps not even twenty years old, he traveled with his friend Germanus to Bethlehem where they joined a monastery.

One day, while standing in the Cave of the Nativity, John and Germanus vowed to go to Egypt. The monasteries of Egypt were reputed to be the most disciplined in the world, the best place for a young man like John to get closer to God like that first Christian ascetic John the Baptist. But some time passed and still they remained in Bethlehem. Then a monk named Pinufius appeared at their door.

Pinufius was an esteemed abbot who had abandoned his monastery in the Nile Delta because he felt over-esteemed by his fellow monks. He believed earthly praise would deny him his heavenly reward because it diminished his humility. In Bethlehem, Pinufius disguised his true identity and was accepted as a beginner and a novice to the monastery in which John and Germanus were living; and there he humbly labored until his identity was revealed by a visiting monk from Egypt. John and Germanus were awestruck at the revelation that Pinufius was an esteemed holy man; and once again they felt drawn to the desert of Egypt, to a land where men like Pinufius were said to walk with God. As for Pinufius, he had abandoned his monastery once before. And just as before, his monks found him and again hauled him home.

John and Germanus soon received permission from their abbot to make a short visit to Egypt. Their short visit lasted seven years. When they finally returned to Bethlehem, they stayed only for a brief time before again departing for Egypt; and there they remained for several years more. All in all, John and Germanus spent some fifteen years in the monasteries of Egypt. Then, around the year 399, they were driven out of Egypt by the bishop of Alexandria for following the teachings of the third-century theologian Origen.

The Egyptian theologian Origen was one of the founders of Christian Platonism. He studied philosophy under the same teacher as the pagan philosopher Plotinus. He taught, among other things, that God is incorporeal and that much of the Bible should be read as allegory rather than literal fact. Augustine learned both of these concepts from Ambrose who, in turn, learned them from reading Origen. Origen also taught that human souls preexisted creation and fell into physical bodies as a consequence of separating from God, an idea with which Ambrose and Augustine strongly disagreed. When John and Germanus were driven out of Egypt for believing God was pure spirit without a physical body, they were following the teaching of Origen. But the simple monks of Egypt would have none of it. They insisted that God must have a physical body because man was made in God's image (or were the monks making God in their image?). Bishop Theophilus of Alexandria agreed with the simple monks and, at their behest, he set upon persecuting John's confreres.

In the wake of the persecutions, John and Germanus fled the Egyptian desert for Constantinople. Fortunately for John Cassian and his friend Germanus, the bishop of Constantinople, John Chrysostom, was sympathetic toward the Origenist monks. John Chrysostom was the bishop of Constantinople from 398 to 404. Chrysostom means golden-mouthed. He was posthumously given the Greek name Chrysostom because of the grand sermons he gave during his lifetime. But in life he was known simply as John. John Cassian and Germanus became his disciples and stayed in Constantinople for five years.

John and Germanus had been living in Constantinople for several years when Chrysostom was cast into exile by the emperor Arcadius. Arcadius ruled the eastern half of the Roman Empire from Constantinople, while his brother Honorius ruled the western half of the empire from Milan. Arcadius exiled John Chrysostom from the empire partially because he held Origenist beliefs in opposition to Catholic orthodoxy, but also because Chrysostom's golden mouth insulted Arcadius' wife. Evidently, the empress believed Chrysostom's preaching against extravagant dress was directed at her. In plain language, she thought he said she dressed like a whore. As Chrysostom's trusted disciple, John Cassian traveled to Rome to plead Chrysostom's case before the pope. And in turn, the pope attempted to intercede with the emperor on Chrysostom's behalf. Yet in the end it was to no avail. Hell hath no fury like a woman's scorn. Even the pope couldn't save Chrysostom from the wrath of Arcadius' wife. Arcadius couldn't budge and Chrysostom died in exile three years later in 407.

John Cassian was likely in Rome when Arcadius' brother Honorius let the city fall to Alaric in 410. By that time, Germanus had died and John was left to roam the world alone. Nobody knows where John went between the years 410 and 419. He might have returned to Constantinople or to Bethlehem. Alternatively, he might have gone to Gaul. In any event, he resurfaced in southern Gaul in the year 419, in the port city of Massilia, which is known today as Marseilles. There he hoped to live in a monastery as he had lived in the monasteries of Egypt.

But Cassian didn't like what he found in the monasteries of Gaul, believing the monks there were less disciplined and less dedicated to God than the monks of Egypt. So he founded two monasteries of his own in Marseilles and, determined to save the monks of Gaul from their errant ways, he wrote two books known, respectively, as the *Institutes* and the *Conferences*. The *Institutes* is a manual on how to organize and run a monastery, while the *Conferences* is a manual containing the teachings the monks must learn and live. With these two books, John Cassian almost single-handedly brought the Christianity of the Egyptian monasteries to the West.

Yet what was so radically different and revolutionary about John's Christianity? What slipped into the Western Empire that was of such great import? The answer is penance. John Cassian brought the monastic practice of confession and penance from east to west, from the Egyptian desert to the port city of Marseille. His *Institutes* and *Conferences* quickly found favor with the monks of Marseille; and from there, his ideas were adopted by the monasteries of Italy, Britain, and Gaul. It is safe to say that confession and penance became a way of life for the monks of the Western Roman Empire thanks to John Cassian. But that's only half of the story.

John Cassian died in Gaul in the year 435, a mere five years after Augustine died in Roman Africa in 430. And in the decades following Cassian's death, St. Patrick and his fellow missionaries would train at the monasteries of Britain and Gaul, where they would learn John Cassian's brand of monasticism. And they would bring John Cassian's brand of monasticism to Ireland, including the practice of repeatedly confessing one's sins and doing penance, where it would take on an entirely new and unexpected dimension. Something special was about to happen in Ireland. A strange brew of Augustine's theology and Egyptian monasticism was about to come together on the Emerald Isle.

For the first five centuries of the Christian faith, mainstream Christianity didn't offer its followers a formal way to have their sins forgiven after they were baptized. In fact, Christians couldn't even agree if sinning after baptism was a normal part of Christian life. After all, if Christ died for man's sins, then why would men keep sinning after baptism? The only people who were confessing their sins and doing penance on a regular basis were monks in monasteries. And for everyone else, there was something called public penance.

Public penance was a one-time shot at forgiveness specifically for the sins of murder, idolatry, and fornication. These sins were considered so serious as to constitute a break with God, and public penance was a kind of second baptism that could mend the break. As its name suggests, public penance was performed in public, usually in front of a church at certain times of the year, and it often took years to complete. A Catholic layman in Rome who was guilty of, say, fornication might spend years praying on the steps of his local church to atone for his sin. Even emperors weren't above doing public penance. In the year 390, when Emperor Theodosius I slaughtered some 7,000 innocent people at Thessalonica, Ambrose excommunicated him until the emperor did public penance to atone for his sin. The actual penance was simple enough. Bishop Ambrose directed the emperor to appear daily at the Church in Milan, get on his knees, and beg forgiveness from God for ordering the massacre of so many innocent people. Yet seeing as he was the emperor, Ambrose went easy on him. He made Theodosius do the penance for only eight months instead of the next twenty years.

Although public penance had been widely practiced by Christians in the Roman Empire, it never became common practice in Ireland. Instead, from their monasteries at the westernmost edge of the world, the monks of Ireland would take a different approach to sin and forgiveness. They would take the monastic practice of confession and penance out of the monasteries and make it available to everyone on the island. Now confession and penance would be for everyone, not only monks in monasteries; and it would be for every kind of sin, not only murder, idolatry, and fornication; and it could be performed as many times as needed, not only once like public penance. The monks would make penance available to the Irish people, and the Irish people would take to it like ducks to water. It was an astonishing development that never could have happened in the Roman Empire. The Romans simply didn't possess the key to making it happen, for the key was something unique to Irish civilization. The key, as it turned out, was Irish law and culture.

Embedded in Irish civilization, there was a difference that made all the difference in the world. The difference was that Irish culture and its laws were more forgiving than Roman law and culture. Whereas a crime in ancient Rome was considered an offense against the emperor and his laws, a crime in ancient Ireland was considered an offense against the person who was harmed. This made a tremendous difference in how crimes were punished.

A crime in ancient Rome was punished severely with death or exile or enslavement. For example, two thieves were crucified alongside Jesus. They got the death penalty just for stealing. The ancient Romans didn't incarcerate criminals as we do today. In stark contrast to the modern penitentiary, Roman prisons were merely places where criminals waited to die.

Irish law and culture, however, was very different from that of Rome. Satisfaction for most crimes in ancient Ireland could be had if the offender paid his victim's "honor price." Each person in Irish society was assigned a value according to his or her social status. This value was known as an honor price. Under this system of law, a king had a very high honor price while a peasant had a very low honor price. Also, a warrior had a greater honor price than an artisan or a farmer; and a man generally had a higher honor price than a woman. The ancient Irish didn't coin money like the Romans. A person's wealth was measured by his possessions and his honor price. So honor prices were typically paid in some kind of valuable commodity like gold, silver, or cattle. For example, if a warrior wrongfully killed a farmer, he had to pay his victim's family both a fine for the murder and the farmer's honor price. Here the warrior might have paid the family in some quantity of silver or milk cows. Additionally, the warrior might have been required to work the land for a period of time if the family was unable to do so. The ancient Irish still reserved the death penalty for certain crimes like killing a king or if the offender couldn't pay his victim's honor price. But it was a very different approach to crime and punishment than in the Roman world.

It didn't take very long for the Irish monks to apply this same concept to their faith. Irish law almost always afforded the guilty a chance to make amends and restore their standing in society. So it seemed only natural to Christians in Ireland that sinners be afforded this same opportunity too. By the middle of the sixth century, Irish monks had assigned honor prices to God in handbooks called penitentials. The penitentials were handbooks that listed common sins and their corresponding penances. For example, the penitential of a sixth-century monk named Finnian lists, among others, the following sin and its price:

If any layman with a wife of his own has intercourse with his female slave, the procedure is this: the female slave is to be sold, and he himself shall not have intercourse with his own wife for an entire year.

Notably, these handbooks were meant to be applied to the clergy and laity alike on an ongoing basis for the forgiveness and healing of sin. Now not only were the monks doing penance, but the farmer and the blacksmith were doing penance too! Many such handbooks were written in the Early Middle Ages. In fact, it was not uncommon for a monastery to develop its own penitential to meet the special needs of its community.

Yet even the monks who wrote these handbooks didn't realize just how radically the penitentials changed the way Catholics experienced their faith. The penitentials introduced something new into the Roman Catholic experience—the freedom to choose between good and evil. Incredibly, mainstream Christianity didn't offer this choice to the average person until the monks of Ireland introduced the penitentials.

The average Catholic in ancient Rome had a peculiar take on free will, one that seems foreign to us today. He believed that his will became linked to God's will through baptism; and that his good works were merely an extension of God's will. On the other hand, he believed that all unbaptized people were sinners because they were separated from God. In his view, even their good acts were sinful because they were done for recognition or for self-satisfaction. The underlying premise here is that the sacrament of baptism connects people to God. Therefore, cut off from goodness itself, the unbaptized had no choice but to live selfish, sinful lives. In the absence of God, selfishness or original sin was the human condition. There was no freedom to choose between good and evil.

In short, a Catholic in ancient Rome denied that he had the freedom to choose between good and evil because he believed men either acted in conformity with God's will through baptism in Christ or they didn't. St. Augustine, who was by far and away the most influential thinker of his time, was the man most responsible for developing this idea through his doctrines of original sin and grace. The idea came to be known as the total depravity of man and it was central to Augustine's doctrine of original sin. Augustine saw sin as an addiction. He believed that human beings were powerless over sin in much the same way an alcoholic is powerless over alcohol. According to Augustine, the only thing that could break men free of their hopelessly selfish condition was God's divine help or grace. In the wake of Augustine's win over Pelagius in 418, these ideas were given the force of Roman law and Church doctrine.

In the year 426, certain monasteries in Italy and Gaul started to oppose Augustine's belief in the total depravity of man using John Cassian's teachings on free will. In the monks' view, Augustine's doctrine rendered their way of life meaningless. If men couldn't freely choose to do right or wrong, then why were the monks doing penance? Contrition, confession, and penance made sense only if men had a choice.

The monks in Italy failed to overturn Augustine's doctrines, and the Church formally condemned John's teachings on free will about a century later in 529. Worse yet, John Cassian was wrongfully labeled a semi-Pelagian in the sixteenth and seventeenth centuries during another theological dispute, a label that has dogged his memory to the present day. John Cassian and the monks he influenced were not Pelagians.

John never rejected the doctrines of original sin and God's grace as Pelagius had done. He merely believed there was a modicum of goodness within men that could impel them on the path to eternal life. John had observed that sometimes a man could set himself upon the path to salvation by an act of free will. However, he also acknowledged that a man couldn't hope to complete that path without God's grace. In John's words, "...sometimes first beginnings of a good will arise, which however cannot attain to the complete performance of what is good unless it is guided by the Lord...."

For the average Christian in Rome, life without penance wasn't easy. Augustine presented sin as an addiction; and the faithful were like recovering addicts who spent their waking hours trying hard not to relapse. Truly, it was a very difficult way of life, one that compelled Roman Catholics of the era to focus on avoiding sin instead of doing good. Like a recovering addict, avoiding sin replaced positive achievement as the focus of their lives.

Consequently, it was not uncommon for Christians to postpone baptism until they were well into adulthood. A Catholic layman in ancient Rome might have sown his wild oats for years before taking the pledge. The idea was to get all of the sinning out of your system before baptism, like Mardi Gras before Lent. Even Augustine, who was a sex addict, postponed baptism. He famously begged God, "Give me chastity and continency, only not yet!"

After baptism, Christians focused on safeguarding their sanctity by withdrawing from public life and turning inward. Most still went about their daily lives, but they stopped caring about worldly problems like corruption in government, abuses of power, the decline of public morals, and barbarian invasions.

On top of this, they believed that the end of the world was at hand. Thus they became more concerned with the afterlife instead of the here and now. And their apathy toward public life contributed mightily to the fall of the Roman Empire.

But Ireland was different. With the advent of the penitentials, Christians in Ireland had the freedom to choose to do good or to go the other way and do penance for their sins. Indeed, the penitentials were predicated on this freedom to choose. After all, penance is for the guilty; and guilt is imputed only to those who can freely choose between right and wrong. Importantly, however, this freedom to choose good was not a way for Christians to save themselves or earn their way into heaven by doing good deeds. It was a component of faith. The Irish were orthodox Catholics. They believed men came to God through faith in Christ and not simply by leading morally upright lives. Yet at the same time, having the freedom to choose between good and evil meant that faith required more than mere belief in Christ. Faith also required a show of faith. It wasn't enough for Christians to talk the talk. They also had to walk the walk because, as the Bible says, faith without works is dead.

Christians in Ireland felt compelled to live their faith not only by going to mass, but also by emulating Christ in their daily lives. Otherwise, the freedom to choose between good and evil meant nothing. This was, in fact, how they integrated penance into Augustine's Catholicism. It was how they added free will to Augustinism. Augustine held that God was the source of good. So the Irish monks reasoned that choosing good meant choosing God. However, this actually meant choosing Christ because in Christianity no one comes to the Father except through the Son. And, in the context of doing penance, choosing Christ meant more than mere belief. It required action. It required that men imitate Christ. Thus the focus of Christian life in Ireland was very different from what it had been in ancient Rome. Whereas Christians in ancient Rome had focused on avoiding sin in order to safeguard their sanctity, Christians in Ireland focused on doing good by imitating the life of Christ as described in the Gospels. In time, this would become more important than anyone could fathom. Soon what started for a handful of Irish monks as a new approach to sin and forgiveness would spark medieval Europe's great monastic movement. Moreover, in the hands of another Irishman just a few hundred years later, it would alter the prevailing model of the cosmos in Western Europe. It would bring St. Augustine's models of heaven and earth together in a single image. And in turn, this would set Christian Europe on the path to our modern world. But all of that was yet to come.

For the time being, Christians in Ireland were more concerned with living their faith than exploring abstract philosophical ideas. And the fullest way to live the faith was to join a monastery. So it should come as no surprise that the sixth century saw monasticism spread throughout Ireland like wildfire. The first developed, brick and mortar monasteries appeared in Ireland around the years 535-540; and by the middle of the sixth century, the monastery was well on its way to becoming the primary religious institution in Ireland. From about the middle of the sixth century on, Ireland saw an explosion of monastic foundations in places like Clonard, Moville, Bangor, Durrow, Derry, Clommacnoise, Lismore, Armagh, Kells, and many more. These monasteries became great centers of learning and scholarship, achieving renown as some of the best schools in Europe during the Middle Ages.

They achieved such prestige that kings and nobles from all over Western Europe sent their sons to be educated in Ireland. Like the penitentials, the monastic schools were the offspring of the marriage between Christianity and Irish civilization. Monasteries had always provided clerical training. But the Irish went further. They established renowned schools at their monasteries by also including secular learning like philosophy and literature. Education and learning had been sacred functions among the ancient Irish. In their tradition, all knowledge was sacred. The ancient Irish priestly classes of *druïdh* (druids), *filidh* (poets, seers), and *baird* (bards) were the keepers of knowledge. Because Ireland had a pre-literate, oral tradition, they spent years memorizing everything from family lineages to epic poems. The education of a *filidh*, for example, lasted at least seven years. The length of their education underscored the importance of their knowledge. Their knowledge formed the very identity of their people, the foundation of their civilization. And they were meticulous in passing it down to their students without deviation from generation to generation. So when the Irish began converting to Christianity, the monks decided that they too would act as the keepers of knowledge by establishing scriptoriums, libraries and monastic schools. Indeed, the Irish monks of this era would produce the oldest vernacular literature in Europe as well as some of the finest illuminated manuscripts ever made, like the Book of Kells and the Lindisfarne Gospels. For along with Christianity, the Irish received the Roman alphabet, reading, writing, and Greek and Roman knowledge. The schools complemented the monastic program very well. In the field of education, the monks' quest to become more Christ-like readily translated as a quest for wisdom and understanding.

The penitentials also spawned a new kind of monk—the *peregrinus pro Christo* or pilgrim for Christ. These monks initiated the great European monastic movement by journeying out of the monastery to walk in the footsteps of Christ. With the advent of the penitentials, the monks had a new obligation to bring Christ's forgiveness to the people. After all, Christ came to earth to save men's souls. Accordingly, the pilgrims for Christ would embark on intrepid quests in foreign lands to spread the gospel, forgive sins, and serve mankind selflessly as Christ had done on earth. They saw Christianity as a vehicle of God's grace; and where people couldn't come to the monastery, they would bring the Irish monastery to the people. And so the monastery became the vehicle by which this new approach to the faith was spread to Britain and the continent. One of the first pilgrims for Christ was an Irish monk named Columba.

In the year 563, on a day when the winds were good for sailing, twelve men and a monk named Columba crowded into a *curach* and pushed off of the east coast of Ireland, into the cold waters of the North Atlantic. Their *curach* was a sailing craft of ancient Irish design. The traditional boat of their ancestors, the *curach* had a wooden frame with skins pulled tightly around it. The seams were then sealed with tar to make the boat waterproof and, finally, a mast was erected at its center to hold the sail. To the medieval mind, pushing off of the Irish coast was like pushing off the end of the earth. Ireland was literally the end of the world in the year 563, but not because men believed the world was flat. Greek and Roman scholars had known the earth was round since ancient times. But they believed the world beyond Ireland was too cold for human habitation. Furthermore, nobody knew the size of the Atlantic Ocean or that the Americas lay on the other side. It seemed a ship's crew might run out of food and water before making it across the globe. With this world in mind, the men sailed north toward the Hebrides, lapping the waves in their boat made of wood and skins and courage and imagination, until they reached the Kingdom of the Dál Riata. The Kingdom of the Dál Riata was an Irish kingdom that occupied most of western Scotland in the Early Middle Ages. They were one of two peoples who settled in ancient Scotland. The other people were called the Picts. The Picts had been in Scotland for centuries and were probably of Celtic origin. But whereas the Irish of the Dál Riata were Christians, the Picts were pagans. Now Columba came as a pilgrim for Christ to convert the Picts, his most precious cargo being the Christianity he carried from Ireland.

Columba was born to royalty in the year 521, a member of one of the most powerful ruling dynasties in Ireland—the O'Neill. Legend has it that an angel appeared to Columba's mother before he was born and told her, "Woman, grieve not, for you shall bring forth a son, who will guide innumerable souls to heaven, and be counted among the prophets of the Most High." Yet nobody knows if he was born a Christian. He might have been born a pagan, taking the name Columba (Latin for dove) at baptism. At some point, Columba was sent to be raised by a foster father. The ancient Irish often sent their children to be raised by foster parents as a way of building alliances between unrelated families. His foster father was a priest named Cruithnechán and Columba likely began his religious training at this time. Later, as a teen, he was sent to study with a poet or druid named Gemmán who taught him "divine wisdom." And when the time came for Columba to train for the clergy, he trained with a priest named Finnian at the monastic school in Clonard or Moville. This Finnian was possibly the same monk who wrote one of the earliest penitentials. But all of this was merely preparation for what would be the defining act of the saint's life.

At the age of forty-two, Columba and twelve of his disciples pushed off from the coast of present-day Northern Ireland in their *curach* and sailed for the Kingdom of the Dál Riata. The reasons for his pilgrimage are shrouded in legend. There are, in fact, multiple versions of the same story. The most colorful version of the story, however, holds that Columba journeyed to Scotland because he was exiled from Ireland for killing scores of men over a book. As the legend goes, Columba had made a hand copy of a Psalter from an original owned by the monk Finnian. Finnian then tried to take Columba's copy, arguing that because the original belonged to him, the copy also belonged to him. Columba naturally objected and, in the Irish tradition, the argument got so heated that it led to the fierce battle of Cúl Dreimne. During the battle, Columba was said to have killed so many men that the Church threatened to excommunicate him until a saint intervened on his behalf. The saint's intercession won Columba the mercy of the Church, and the Church ordered him into exile in Britain in lieu of excommunication. And there he was to convert as many men to Christianity as he had killed at the battle of Cúl Dreimne as penance for his sins. While we may want to believe this captivating tale, it is mostly a legend that was designed to make Christian monks out of pagan Irish warriors. It was a kind of advertisement for the Church aimed at the warrior class of ancient Irish society. We may never know exactly what crossed

Columba's mind before he crossed the sea to Britain. But what happened when he got there is another story.

Columba first landed in the kingdom of Conall mac Comgaill, king of the Dál Riata. It was an auspicious time for Columba to make the trip because his family's star was on the rise. Ancient Ireland was divided into five provinces: Ulster, Munster, Leinster, Connacht, and Meath. Each province was ruled by a king; and under each provincial king, there were many client kings who ruled much smaller kingdoms within the province. This was why Ireland had hundreds of kings. The province of Meath was the seat of the high king, the king to whom the other four provincial kings owed their allegiance, and the O'Neill dynasty held this seat. Now Columba's kinsmen had already won the battle of Cúl Dreimne two years earlier, putting them in line for the O'Neill high kingship back in Ireland. This meant that Conall mac Comgaill would be more willing to accommodate Columba and his monks because of Columba's family connections. Once among the Dál Riata, Columba was able to persuade the king to grant him the island of Iona, in the Hebrides, on which to build his monastery.

Located in the middle of the Irish-speaking world, Iona was an ideal location for Columba. It offered equal access by sea to Ireland, the Kingdom of the Dál Riata, and the land of the Picts. To the west lay Ireland; and to the east lay the Kingdom of the Dál Riata; and to the northeast lay the land of the Picts. Columba's monastery soon became a hub for Christianity in the Irish-speaking world. It even achieved renown on the continent for its school, which had earned a reputation as one of the best in Europe. But the real jewel in Iona's crown was its missionary work. From Iona, Columba and his monks brought

Christianity and the penitentials to nearly all of Britain. At first, their success won them many friends. Then, as is often the case, it made them many enemies.

Columba's mission to the Picts, in the land that would become Scotland, began with their king, Bruide. There is a famous story that tells how Columba gained entry into King Bruide's fortress. Having spent hours climbing the steep hill to its approach, the saint had finally arrived at the colossal gates of the king's fortress. There he stood at the gates and waited; and he waited until it became clear that the king, swelled with pride, refused to acknowledge him as God's humble servant. Columba approached the gates with his monks and made the sign of the cross. Then he knocked three times, one knock each for the Father, the Son, and the Holy Spirit. At once the gates flung open! The king was humbled before the power of almighty God and from that day forward he welcomed Columba in peace and honor. While this story is more legend than history, it is likely that Columba did indeed convert Bruide. Like Patrick, Columba attempted to win over kings as a way of winning over their subjects. And like Patrick, we may never know exactly how he did it. But certainly we know that Scotland received Christianity from the Irish.

When Columba died in the year 597, those who knew him already believed he was a saint. He had established several monasteries in Ireland and Scotland; and he had initiated the long process of converting the Picts to Christianity, a process that would continue for decades after his death. Now his successors would bring Irish Christianity to the English by winning over kings and commoners alike.

The story of how the Irish brought Christianity to the English is riveting, partly because it is so rarely heard. It is popularly believed that the Church in Rome converted the pagan English to Christianity. A large part of the problem arises from the sources, particularly an English monk named Bede. When St. Bede completed his *Ecclesiastical History of the English People* around the year 731, he thought it was better for the Church in England to look as though it had received the faith directly from the Church in Rome because the Irish had been accused of teaching false doctrine. So he exaggerated Rome's contribution by downplaying the Irish contribution. It wasn't intentional, but just a bias. Subsequently, Bede's treatise went on to become a major source for English history and Rome got the credit due the Irish. The telltale sign that the English received Christianity from the Irish, however, was the prevalence of the penitentials in the English Church.

After the Roman Empire abandoned Britain, the Angles, Saxons, and Jutes settled in the southern half of the island. These were the pagan, Germanic peoples who would eventually become the English prior to the Norman conquest of England in 1066. In 598, Rome sent a bishop named Augustine to Britain to evangelize the English. He settled in Canterbury, in the south of England, and from there he made some progress in converting the English to Christianity. But within a short time after his death in 604, his mission collapsed. Rome would continue to support the mission of Canterbury; and Canterbury would go on to become the seat of the Church in England. But it would never achieve widespread success in converting the English. It would fail for the same reason Palladius and his immediate successors failed to convert the Irish on a grand scale—the bishops from Rome just didn't understand the people. On the other hand, the Irish understood the English quite well, which greatly accounted for their success in spreading Christianity in England from north to south. And it all began on a small island off the coast of northeast England called Lindisfarne.

The Irish monks acquired Lindisfarne when the English king of Bernicia was killed in battle. His sons Oswald and Oswiu had been exiled to Iona years earlier and were converted to Christianity there. When their father died in 633, Oswald returned to England from his exile on Iona; and there he became a powerful Christian king, ruling most of Northumbria, parts of Dál Riata, and Pictland as well. Yet he had a problem: most of his subjects were pagans. So, in order to strengthen the unity of his kingdom, he brought in an Irish monk from Iona named Aidan to convert them to Christianity. Thus Aidan was made bishop and King Oswald gave him the island of Lindisfarne, off the northeast coast of England, on which to build a monastery.

The island of Lindisfarne sits in a dramatic bay which floods at high tide as a rush of water comes rolling in from the sea. The island is connected to the mainland by a causeway, just like Mont-St.-Michel off the coast of Normandy. Crossing the causeway at high tide feels a bit like walking on water. Today, its monastery is a ruin that draws tourists instead of monks. But 1,400 years ago, from atop his island monastery, Bishop Aidan united members of rival feuding dynasties under the umbrella of the Christian faith. Aidan enjoyed great success at converting nobles and commoners alike; and England was becoming evermore united in faith, if not in politics.

In 651, the monks of Iona and Lindisfarne had another stroke of luck when King Oswald was killed in battle. His brother Oswiu succeeded him as king and brought the English middle kingdoms of Mercia under his control. This opened the door to a mission there and, as a result, the people of Mercia were converted to Christianity. Then Oswiu persuaded the King of the East Saxons to convert to Christianity. This made it possible for the monks to establish a mission there, too, and the East Saxons adopted the Christian faith of the Irish. Notably, Bishop Aidan and another monk named Fínán spearheaded these efforts, leading the monks of Iona and Lindisfarne into the heart of England.

But success has a way of making enemies as well as friends. And if there was one man leading the charge to stop the success of the Irish monks in England, then it was a Northumbrian nobleman named Wilfrid. Wilfrid was an English cleric who had traveled to Rome and learned the "true faith." That is to say, he learned how things were done in Rome only to return home to England to find the Irish monks doing it differently. Among their offenses, in his view, the Irish celebrated Easter on a date different from that of the Church in Rome and they were wearing the monk's tonsure differently from other Roman Catholics too. The tonsure is that part of a monk's head which is shaved when he enters the monastery as a sign of casting off vanity. The Irish shaved the frontal half of the head while the rest of the Church shaved the crown. While the Irish tonsure might have contravened Roman practice, it wasn't nearly as great a problem as the Easter question. The medieval Church believed that celebrating Easter on the wrong date denied Christians the benefit of Christ's redemption. Hence Wilfrid and his faction truly believed that the Irish monks and all of their converts were going to hell. But in truth, the Irish method of determining the date of Easter wasn't wrong. It was merely older than the method that was then used by Rome.

Wilfrid went after the Irish monks with an almost fanatical determination, working to bring their practices into uniformity with those sanctioned by Rome. But even more troubling, he sought to curtail their autonomy to decide matters like the tonsure and the date of Easter by bringing the monasteries under the more immediate control of Rome. In other words, he wanted to organize the monasteries like diocesan Churches by placing them under the control of English bishops. Wilfrid maneuvered behind the scenes to stop the Irish. He persuaded the king's son that something needed to be done about the monks; and the king's son persuaded the king to convene the infamous Synod of Whitby.

The official reason for the Synod of Whitby in 664 was to bring the Irish Easter and tonsure in line with the Church in Rome. But the real reasons for Whitby were to bring the Irish monks under the control of English bishops and to give the king the power to appoint those bishops. So it should come as no surprise that Whitby wasn't really a synod at all. That is to say, it wasn't a council of bishops. It was a royal council presided over and decided by King Oswiu. The council was convened at the behest of King Oswiu's son, who had fallen in with Wilfrid. Wilfrid used the king's son to convene Whitby and the king used Whitby as an opportunity to secure royal power over the Church. The power to appoint the bishop of the Northumbrian Church had long rested with the abbot of Iona. But by casting his decision in favor of Wilfrid, King Oswiu transferred that power to himself.

But why would the king want the power to appoint his own bishop? The answer was simple. By putting his own man in as bishop, the king made sure he always had the support of the Church. But now, with the king's entry into Church affairs,

Iona's authority to make decisions for churches and monasteries in England was finished. The king wanted his bishops to rule the Church in England, not monks. The change was dramatic. Irish monasteries and the people whom they served were typically governed by their founding houses, which is why Iona in the Hebrides governed Lindisfarne on the Northumbrian coast. But now the Church in England would be governed by bishops who presided over dioceses, as had been the system on the continent since the days of the Roman Empire. Now churches would be governed according to location, not affiliation, by local bishops who enforced the practices of the Roman Church. The diocesan church would now supplant the monastery as the primary religious institution in Britain.

It seemed a fatal blow to Irish Christianity in England. Yet astonishingly, despite Wilfrid's success at breaking the power of the Irish monks there, despite his fierce opposition to the Irish Easter and tonsure, the penitentials went unchallenged! The most radical innovation of the Irish Church, the thing that should have met the most resistance from Wilfrid's anti-Irish faction in England, wasn't recognized as an innovation at all. The penitentials and all that went with them remained hidden in plain view from Wilfrid and his cabal, disguised as a part of everyday Christian life. But unfortunately for the Irish, the Synod of Whitby denied them credit for their substantial contribution to English culture by making it seem like their only contribution was the nonconforming tonsure and a wrong date for Easter.

Despite their defeat at Whitby, the Irish monks remained forever true to their calling. Indeed, the pinnacle of their achievements came more than three decades after Whitby with the passage of the world's first humanitarian law—the

Law of Innocents. The Law of Innocents was the brainchild of the ninth abbot of Iona, an Irish monk named Adomnán who shepherded the great monastery from 679 until his death in 704. Among Adomnán's many achievements were his *Life of St. Columba* and his Law of Innocents. His *Life of St. Columba* is a hagiography, which is a biography of the saint's life replete with stories of his miracles and his gift for prophecy. But perhaps even more remarkable than his hagiography of Columba was Adomnán's Law of Innocents. Also known as the Law of Adomnán, it was the first law of its kind, prohibiting violence against women, children, and churches during warfare—a kind of Geneva Convention for the Middle Ages.

The passage of the law in 697 at a grand council in Ireland was itself an extraordinary event. Leaders from both the Church and the state came from as far away as Dál Riata and Pictland to pass the first Church law to bind the clergy and laity alike. At the heart of the world's first human rights law was an idea straight out of Irish Christianity, the imitation of Christ. Showing compassion for non-combatants during warfare certainly was in keeping with the example of Christ even if war itself wasn't. Like the penitentials, the Law of Innocents had no precedent in human history. It was truly the first of its kind, a remarkable leap forward for all of humanity.

In the almost century and a half between the founding of Iona in 563 and Adomnán's death in 704, Irish Christianity—that form of orthodox Christianity characterized by penance, free will, and the imitation of Christ—replaced paganism as the dominant religion in Britain and Ireland. Such a sweeping and dramatic change in such a short period of time is extraordinary in its own right. But perhaps even more surprising was the fact that, during the entire conflict between the Irish monks and Wilfrid's anti-Irish faction in Britain, the peculiarly Irish penitential system was never challenged. Consequently, Irish Christianity became a fully integrated part of the English and Scottish Churches from their inceptions. Yet Britain and Ireland weren't the only lands to receive this gift, this Secret Gospel of Ireland. Around the same time that Columba was preaching to the Picts, another Irish monk set off across the sea to bring the penitentials to the rest of Europe. He wasn't the first Irish *peregrinus* to establish monasteries on the continent, but he was the most influential. For continental Europe, the arrival of an Irish monk named Columbanus heralded the dawn of a new day.

CHAPTER FOUR
How the Irish Invaded Europe

n the year 610, the most dangerous man in the Western world was a seventy-year-old Irish monk named Columbanus. He was so dangerous that the king of Burgundy condemned him to exile back in Ireland. The old abbot, however, was so loved by his disciples that every monk in the land threatened to follow Columbanus into exile. But the king wouldn't allow it. King Theuderic couldn't afford to lose the monks. In medieval Europe, a monastery was like a church, a hospital, and a school all rolled into one. The king needed the monks to serve his people far more than the monks needed the king to protect them. So the king declared that only Columbanus' fellow Irishmen were allowed to follow their master into exile. For now it seemed that King Theuderic had rid the continent of the terrible Irish.

And so it happened one somber day that the king's soldiers took Columbanus and his fellow Irishmen from their monastery at Luxeuil, on the slope of the Vosges Mountains in eastern France, and delivered them to the French seaport of Nantes. There, at the mouth of the Loire River, the Irish monks were loaded into a small boat bound for the land where they were born. As the boat made its way through the harbor and into the open waters of the Atlantic, Columbanus prayed for deliverance from exile. To return to Ireland was to depart from the path of Christ, for he was a *peregrinus pro Christo*—a lifelong pilgrim determined to follow in the footsteps of Christ in a foreign land. So on the deck of that boat, Columbanus humbly bowed before God and prayed that no earthly power be allowed to stand in the way of his salvation by knocking him off the path of Christ. God must have heard the old monk that day because what happened next was a miracle of the most extraordinary kind, a miracle that had been in the making since the day Columbanus was born some seventy years earlier.

Around the year 540, on a stretch of land in Ireland between the Rivers Slaney and Barrow, a child was born who would become a saint. The Latin form of his name was Columbanus. But he was born *Colum-ban*, which is Irish for the fair Colum, because he was so beautiful. Legend has it that his beauty was nearly his ruin. In his adolescence, he was besieged by the favor of many young and beautiful women that were, all of them, descendants of Eve—descendants of that long line of Old Testament vixens that caused the fall of many a great man beginning with Adam. They endeavored to lead the fair Colum away from God and into a life of carnal pleasures. Torn by temptation, the boy sought the advice of an old woman hermit who lived in the nearby woods. She warned him of the power of women and the weakness of the flesh, and then she sent him away. Columbanus returned to the world and, with the Gospels in one hand and a sword in the other, he fended off his temptresses, went straight home to his mother, and said goodbye. Columbanus had succeeded where Adam had failed, and off to the monastery he went.

Columbanus said goodbye to his mother and journeyed to Lough Erne, which today is two lakes on the River Erne. There, embraced by the waters of the Erne, sat an island called Cluain Inis; and on the island was a monastery founded by an abbot named Sinell. Sinell had been schooled by Finnian at the famous monastery at Clonard. And just as Sinell had been taught by his master Finnian many years earlier at Clonard, so too would Sinell teach Columbanus at his monastery on Cluain Inis. Columbanus might have already learned to read and write some Latin from the family Psalter back home, but his formal education began here. It was his first taste of the monastic life. Nobody knows how long Columbanus spent at Cluain Inis. But it couldn't have been too many years because Sinell died while Columbanus was still quite young. After Sinell died, Columbanus left Cluain Inis for the monastery at Bangor, where he continued his training for the clergy.

The monastery at Bangor was just three years old when Columbanus arrived. Its abbot and founder, Comgall, became Columbanus' teacher, instructing him in Latin and Irish, the Bible, Augustine, Cassian, Virgil, Horace, and Ausonius, just to name a few. It was around this time also that the Irish monks began to write down Ireland's oral tradition to create Europe's oldest vernacular literature. Columbanus excelled at all of his duties to become the most esteemed monk and scholar at the monastery. He was ordained a priest at Bangor and settled into the rhythm of monastic life, into the steady rhythm of prayer, penance, fasting, scholarship, teaching, manual labor, pastoral care, and bodily mortification. Any other monk might have struggled for a lifetime attempting to master the rigors of monastic life, yet Columbanus did it with ease. For him, a life of obedience and deprivation at Bangor had become too comfortable, too predictable, too routine. And a life without struggle was not the path of Christ.

Columbanus urged the abbot to let him go into the world as a pilgrim for Christ, into a foreign land to live selflessly among its people. The old abbot Comgall refused Columbanus' request. To lose the most esteemed monk at the monastery would be a terrible loss for Bangor. After all, Columbanus would likely succeed Comgall as abbot. Furthermore, there were few monks able to assume Columbanus' duties as teacher and scholar and even fewer still as priest. Only a priest could say mass, administer the sacraments, and administer penance. So that was it, there would be no life as a pilgrim for Columbanus because the monastery needed him. Yet still Columbanus persisted in his pleas to go to the continent as a pilgrim for Christ; and still Comgall continued to say no. Then, for some unknown reason, the abbot changed his mind. Not only did he grant Columbanus' request to follow the path of a *peregrinus pro Christo*, he supplied him with all he needed to get underway, including twelve disciples. And chief among Columbanus' disciples was a monk named Gall.

In the year 590, the winds of change blew for Columbanus. The time had come for him to leave Ireland for the Kingdom of the Franks, to the land that would later become France. As the monks hoisted their sail and slipped from the shores of old Ireland, the old abbot Comgall watched his monks depart like a father watching his sons leave home. Comgall had done all he could to prepare his monks to go into the world. Now they were in God's hands.

Their journey to Francia was blessed with good weather and a fair wind. Legend says they sailed to Cornwall in Britain before finally landing at Saint-Malo on the coast of

Brittany. From there they headed inland on foot and soon made their way to King Guntram of Burgundy, to his royal residence in Chalon-sur-Saône. Guntram was a good king, but like all members of the Merovingian dynasty he had seen his share of suffering. All of his natural born sons had died by murder or disease, a tragedy the king saw as God's punishment for his many sins. And so the king welcomed Columbanus and his monks as a sign of God's salvation. But salvation wasn't the only reason why old Guntram welcomed Columbanus. The monks also brought scholarship and learning, which was very valuable indeed to any medieval European kingdom. Irish monasteries had already established a reputation in Western Europe for running schools of the highest quality. And the Irish monks practiced a purer form of Latin than what was spoken on the continent. The Irish had preserved Latin as a second language just as they had received it from the Romans more than two centuries earlier. On the other hand, the Frankish bishops were by that time speaking a form of Latin that was well on its way to becoming French. Furthermore, the Irish possessed classical Latin texts that were largely unavailable outside of Byzantium. The Byzantine Empire was the continuation of the Eastern Roman Empire after the fall of Rome in 476; and its capital was the magnificent city of Constantinople, which today is called Istanbul. The term "Byzantine Empire" was first used by a German historian in the sixteenth century to distinguish it from the ancient Roman Empire. But the people of the empire never called themselves Byzantines. To each other and the world they were simply Romans. A treasure trove of ancient Greek and Latin texts would later come to Europe through Constantinople and Moorish Spain. But until then, the monasteries would serve as Western Europe's main repositories of books by ancient Greek and Roman authors.

It was, to say the least, serendipitous that Columbanus and his monks should have arrived at Guntram's palace in the year 590. Old King Guntram was near the end of his life and was obsessed with doing charity in order to curry favor with God. So out of charity or guilt, Guntram endowed Columbanus with land on which to build a monastery in the hope that the monks might minister to his people. But Columbanus wasn't going to make things easy for the people or his monks. He believed the more remote the monastery, the better to live like Christ in the desert. So he chose a remote and abandoned Roman settlement in the Vosges Mountains called Annegray. There the monks built a monastery and attempted to be self-sufficient, eating only tree bark, wild herbs, and berries. And, in the great pilgrim tradition, they ended up starving until the nearby monastery of Saulcy sent food.

As the story goes, the abbot of Saulcy had a dream that Columbanus and his monks needed help, so he sent a horse cart filled with food to the Irishmen. The monk who was charged with delivering the food became lost and separated from the horse cart on his way to Annegray, but the horse continued alone and arrived at the monastery just in time to save the day. It was a miracle! Or perhaps not. Columbanus and his monks might just as well have asked for help, which then arrived without incident. Tales of miracles, however, were a very effective form of advertising. Because soon after the monks from Saulcy spread the news of the miracle at Annegray, throngs of the faithful began making pilgrimages to Columbanus' monastery. And conveniently for Saulcy, it also served to split the workload with Annegray by getting people to go a little farther for the services of another monastery.

After news of Columbanus' piety got out, his monastery at Annegray grew by leaps and bounds. But even more importantly, it had attracted the attention of the Frankish aristocracy as a place to send their sons for an education. By winning the favor of a royal official whose son was studying at the monastery, Columbanus was able to secure a grant of land for a second monastery in 594. The site was the abandoned Roman settlement of Lixivium, better known by its French name Luxeuil, eight miles west of Annegray. Luxeuil soon became more crowded and prominent than Annegray, which prompted Columbanus to establish a third monastery three miles to the north at Fontaines. In the space of about five years, Columbanus had established three thriving monasteries at Annegray, Luxeuil, and Fontaines, with the monastery at Luxeuil acting as the motherhouse.

Columbanus' monasteries were places where commoners came to worship, clergy came to follow, noblemen came to learn, the sick came to get well, and everyone came for salvation. Salvation was, in fact, Columbanus' greatest draw. For the men who joined his monasteries, Columbanus offered the uniquely Irish *anam cara*. *Anam cara* is an Irish term that means soul friend. A monk's *anam cara* was his spiritual guide, the person to whom he confessed his sins and to whom he turned for direction and advice. According to Columbanus' Communal Rule, the monks were required to confess their sins twice a day to their *anam cara*. All of which was fine and good for recruiting monks, but it didn't bring in the masses. The public came for something else. They came to have their sins forgiven. Up until this time, the average Catholic layperson in Francia didn't have options for the forgiveness of sins. Indeed, it was the old Roman practice of public penance or nothing at all. So when the people got wind that Columbanus was forgiving sins and doling out penances, they came in droves. It was so popular that other monasteries began to adopt the practice. And just as in Ireland and Britain, penance quickly became a way of life for Catholics in Burgundy. For the monasteries of Annegray, Luxeuil, and Fontaines, forgiving sins really drew in the crowds. Yet unfortunately for Columbanus, his ever-increasing popularity also drew the ire of the local bishops.

Looking back, Columbanus probably should have sought the bishops' permission before founding his monasteries in their dioceses. But it never crossed his mind to do so because monks in Ireland didn't live in dioceses and they didn't answer to bishops. So he proceeded to build his monasteries only on the authority of the king, just as he would have done in Ireland. This was a bad mistake. Eventually, the bishops grew tired of what they perceived as an encroachment on their power and they tried to get rid of him on trumped-up charges. In other words, they went after him for the Irish Easter and tonsure just as the nobleman Wilfrid would do to the Irish in England some sixty years later.

The issue of the Irish tonsure probably could have been resolved quite easily if it hadn't been charged with the far more controversial Easter question. For as long as anyone could remember, there had been division within the Christian faith regarding how to accurately calculate the date of Easter. Getting the date right was very important to the Church. It was believed that Easter had to be celebrated on the date when the resurrection actually happened in order for Christians to get the benefit of Christ's sacrifice on the cross. The controversy stretched back to the days of the Roman Empire when Rome split with Alexandria on the method of determining the correct date of Christ's death and resurrection; and over the centuries, the method for calculating the date of Easter was constantly in flux. As for the Church in Ireland, it settled on a method for calculating the date of Easter early in its history, while the Church in Rome adopted a later method. And this set the stage for conflict on the issue, as happened when Wilfrid challenged the Irish monks in England at the Synod of Whitby in 664. But Whitby was yet to come. For now, the Irish were reluctant to abandon their practice in favor of a newer one because they believed the older method for calculating Easter was closer to what actually happened. So Columbanus was forced to defend himself against the bishops of Burgundy over a date and a haircut.

For his part, Columbanus didn't manage the crisis well at all. When the bishops first made the charges against him in 595, Columbanus responded by appealing directly to Pope Gregory the Great. In the eyes of the bishops he looked impertinent, like he had intentionally flouted their authority to decide the matter. In other words, he appeared to have gone outside of their chain of command. But just as before, the problem was cultural more than anything else. As an Irishman, Columbanus didn't see himself as part of the bishops' hierarchy. Irish monks typically answered to their abbot; and the various abbots answered to the abbot of their motherhouse. But as the abbot of the motherhouse at Luxeuil, the next highest authority to whom Columbanus could appeal on religious matters was the pope himself. The pope, however, was reluctant to take sides and so the dispute went on.

Yet even without the pope's support, Columbanus had friends in high places. He was surrounded by an aura of protection from the Frankish nobility. Columbanus and his monasteries were substantial assets to the nobility. They weren't about to lose schools, hospitals, and churches over a date and a haircut or because of the bishops' wounded pride. All of which explains why the bishops kept coming at Columbanus for the next ten years, again raising the issues of the Irish tonsure and Easter in the years 603, 607, and 610. The pope refused to settle the issue so as not to offend the bishops or the monks. And Columbanus enjoyed the protection of the nobility, which rendered the bishops powerless to take action against him. Yet the status quo wouldn't last forever. The Irishman was about to lose the support of the king over a Merovingian blood feud.

All the while Columbanus was building monasteries and defending his mission against jealous bishops, the throne was changing hands. Old King Guntram, the man who had been so supportive of Columbanus and his mission, died in 592. Then, because all of Guntram's sons had died before him, his nephew Childebert II took the throne of Burgundy. Finally, in the year 596, Childebert II died and the lands of Burgundy and Austrasia were divided between his sons, Theuderic II and Theudebert II. So Theuderic inherited the Kingdom of Burgundy (today, southeastern France and parts of Switzerland), while his brother Theudebert took the Kingdom of Austrasia (today, northeastern France, western Germany, Belgium, Luxembourg, the Netherlands, and parts of Switzerland).

In the division of lands following their father's death, Theuderic also received four lands that were previously Austrasian: the Saintois in the Moselle valley, Alsace, the Thurgau, and Campanensis. Naturally, his brother Theudebert, as King of Austrasia, believed he should have received these lands as part of his inheritance. It was a recipe for disaster. With this division of lands, all of the ingredients for a bloody and destructive feud were there. Yet history wouldn't lay blame for the ensuing savagery on either brother. That distinction would go to the boys' grandmother, the infamous Visigothic queen Brunhild. She was portrayed as the real power behind young King Theuderic's throne, the woman who drove the brothers to war and Columbanus from Burgundy.

Legend has it that Brunhild was a conniving, power-hungry shrew who ruled Burgundy by controlling her grandson Theuderic like a puppet. To this end, she encouraged her grandson to take concubines instead of a wife so there would be no rival queen; and he sired four illegitimate sons by them. As the story goes, Columbanus came to the royal residence one day and was asked by Brunhild to bless Theuderic's four illegitimate sons. But Columbanus refused. "Know that these boys will never bear the royal sceptre," he said, "for they were begotten in sin." Brunhild was so enraged at Columbanus that she let loose her wrath on him. She persuaded her grandson King Theuderic to ride to Luxeuil and demand entry to the inner cloisters of the monastery. To the monks, the inner cloisters of the monastery were sacred spaces like the Holy of Holies in King Solomon's Temple. They were the spaces where the monks communed with God. For the king to force his way inside was an affront to the abbot's authority and a violation of the asceticism that formed the very core of the monks' way of life. And it was all a ruse. Predictably, Columbanus refused the king entry to the monastery. The king knew full well that Columbanus could not let him into the most sacred parts of Luxeuil. And as planned, Theuderic ordered that Columbanus be taken prisoner to the fortress town of Besançon, overlooking the River Doubs, for his "disobedience." Brunhild had thus defeated the Irishman—or so it was written.

But that's not what really happened. What really happened back in 610 was that Theuderic was forced to expel Columbanus from Burgundy because he posed a real threat to Theuderic's rule. Earlier that year, Theudebert forced his brother Theuderic to return the four lands that had previously been Austrasian. This led to war between the brothers, a war in which Theuderic needed the support of the bishops. Theuderic needed the bishops to endorse the legitimacy of his war in order to sell it to the nobility and commoners alike. He needed the bishops to give his war a moral mandate by telling everyone that he was on the side of right. Otherwise he would be seen as just another greedy king who was willing to risk other people's lives for personal gain. But Columbanus was a source of division. Given Columbanus' history with the bishops, the king would never win their support with Columbanus at his side. This was why, in the year 610, the most dangerous man in the Western world was a seventy-year-old Irish monk named Columbanus. As far as King Theuderic was concerned, the Irishman had to go.

History would vilify the name of Brunhild, making her a scapegoat for Merovingian bloodlust and the persecution of Columbanus. As is so often the case, the truth made for bad politics. When the monk Jonas of Susa began writing his *Life of St. Columbanus* some twenty-five years after the Irishman had died, the greatest supporter of the Columbanian monasteries was the Merovingian dynasty. With its support, the monasteries enjoyed protection from the bishops, which enabled them to rapidly establish affiliated houses. To paint the Merovingians as fratricidal warmongers and blame them for the exile of a revered saint was not, to say the least, in the monks' best interests.

The monk Jonas later wrote that Columbanus escaped from Besançon (by a miracle of course) and returned to his monastery at Luxeuil. Unable to control Columbanus, the enraged Theuderic finally ordered Columbanus into exile back in Ireland. Only the Irish monks were allowed to accompany Columbanus back to Ireland. The king didn't want to lose the entire monastery, just the troublemakers. So Columbanus and a group of his Irish disciples, including Gall who had been a member of Columbanus' original twelve monks twenty years earlier, were taken to the French seaport of Nantes and put on a boat. As the boat made its way through the harbor and into the open waters of the Atlantic Ocean, the monks prayed for deliverance from exile. Suddenly, the wind began to blow and churn the dark waters of the sea, forcing the boat to return to its harbor. The captain, fearing God and wanting nothing to do with the holy men, put the monks off of his boat and returned them to freedom. While this colorful story might well be exaggerated for effect, Columbanus and his monks somehow gave their captors the slip and headed inland on foot.

Columbanus and his monks made their way to the Kingdom of Neustria (today, most of northern France, including Paris), to the palace of King Chlothar II. There was no love between Chlothar and his second cousins Theuderic and Theudebert, or their grandmother Brunhild. The colossal skeleton in the Merovingian family closet was that Chlothar's parents, King Chilperic and Queen Fredegund, had murdered Brunhild's sister decades earlier. The story is a tangled web of jealousy, murder, and revenge.

Once upon a time there were three grandsons of the great King Clovis, the Father of France who united Francia under Roman Catholicism in 496 after the fall of Rome. His grandson's were Guntram, Sigibert, and Chilperic. When their father died, all of Francia was divided among them. To Guntram went the Kingdom of Burgundy; to Sigibert went the Kingdom of Austrasia; and to Chilperic went the Kingdom of Neustria.

Brunhild was a stunningly beautiful princess from Visigothic Spain who was given as a bride to King Sigibert. She was so beautiful, in fact, that her beauty made Sigibert's brother Chilperic, king of Neustria, jealous. He was so jealous that he sent for Brunhild's older sister in Spain and married her. Chilperic, however, would never make a faithful husband. He had a wandering eye for mistresses and courtesans, one of whom was a girl named Fredegund. Normally, the king would have had both his wife and the consort. But Brunhild's sister would have none of it. She wanted all mistresses banished from the royal court, especially Fredegund. That's when Chilperic lost interest in Brunhild's sister and desired to marry Fredegund. Yet in those days there was almost no such thing as a divorce. So the king did the next best thing. He conspired with Fredegund to murder his wife so he could marry Fredegund. And so Chilperic and Fredegund had Brunhild's sister strangled to death.

Brunhild went into a rage when she learned that Chilperic and Fredegund had murdered her sister. She vowed to avenge her sister's death by persuading her husband King Sigibert to wage war against his brother Chilperic. But in the course of the war between Austrasia and Neustria, Fredegund had King Sigibert assassinated. From that day forward, Brunhild, who was now a queen without a king, would have to plot her revenge through her son and her grandsons.

In the end, Brunhild never got her revenge. Fredegund escaped Brunhild's wrath and died years later of natural causes. Meanwhile, the other brother, King Guntram of Burgundy, adopted King Sigibert and Brunhilds' son Childebert II in order to inherit the Kingdom of Austrasia. And when Guntram died in 592, Brunhild's son Childebert became king of Burgundy and Austrasia. Finally, Childebert died in 596 and the lands of Austrasia and Burgundy were again divided between his two sons, Theuderic and Theudebert.

As for Chilperic and Fredegund, they had a son named Chlothar II. When Chilperic died in 584, Chlothar became king of Neustria. And given the bad family history between Neustria, Austrasia, and Burgundy, he welcomed Columbanus and his monks as friends, which is to say he welcomed them in the Merovingian tradition as enemies of his enemies. He offered them land within his kingdom on which to build a monastery, but Columbanus declined the offer. Instead, Columbanus wanted to take his disciples eastward into the remote wilderness of the Alps. So Chlothar granted the monks safe passage and they departed.

Columbanus and his disciples journeyed east through Paris and into the Kingdom of Austrasia. They arrived at King Theudebert's court in Metz by way of a friendly courtier named Chagneric whose son was a monk at Luxeuil. Knowing what a blessing Columbanus and his monasteries had been to Theuderic's kingdom, Theudebert offered Columbanus land for a monastery with the promise that it would serve as a base from which to convert neighboring pagans. Now here was a mission worthy of St. Patrick himself, they thought.

Columbanus accepted the offer and set off with his Irish monks for present-day Switzerland. Compliments of the king, they traveled by boat up the Rhine to the shore of Lake Zurich. There they started to build a monastery atop the ruins of an abandoned Roman fort and preach to the native pagans. They were meeting with some success, too, until Gall decided to trash their pagan temples. He truly was well-intentioned, like a wife who trashes her husband's cigarettes to help him break the habit or a husband who throws out all of the junk food to help his wife lose weight. Of course the natives didn't think they had a problem in the first place. After that incident, ill will toward Columbanus and his disciples steadily built until eventually they were run out of town. They headed east from Lake Zurich to the town of Bregenz, at the westernmost edge of present-day Austria, on the shore of Lake Constance. There they built another monastery and, for two years, endeavored to convert the native pagans to Christianity. And they might have stayed for good had they not lost the protection of King Theudebert.

Still stewing over the loss of the four territories to his brother, Theuderic launched a savage war against his brother to recover the lands. Eventually, Theuderic captured his brother Theudebert and interned him in a monastery. But later Theuderic had a change of heart toward his brother, so he yanked him out of the monastery and had Theudebert killed. Then, five or six months later, Theuderic died of dysentery at the Austrasian capital of Metz.

Never one to miss an opportunity, Chlothar raised an army to seize both the thrones of Austrasia and Burgundy and

unite all of Francia under one king. Brunhild attempted to raise an army to resist Chlothar, son of her mortal enemies Chilperic and Fredegund, but the nobility turned on her and sided with Chlothar. Chlothar took her prisoner and had the seventy-year-old Brunhild stripped naked and displayed on a camel's back for three days. At the end of the three days, the old woman was tied to wild horses by her hair, hands, and feet. Then the horses were sent galloping in opposite directions until nothing was left of the old queen but the pieces of her bloodied corpse.

Theudebert's death meant the end for Columbanus and his monks at Bregenz. They had lived there in peace only because they enjoyed the protection of the king. Now that the king was gone, the pagans were free to oppose the monks openly for trying to destroy their gods. The pagans first convinced a local nobleman, Duke Gunzo, to banish Columbanus and his monks from Bregenz. Then, in case the monks didn't get the message, the pagans lured two monks into the forest using a stolen cow as bait and murdered them. Columbanus had no choice but to leave. He ordered his monks to follow him out of Bregenz and all of them obeyed Columbanus except for his most beloved monk Gall. When the time came to leave the monastery at Bregenz, Gall was stricken with a severe illness and couldn't travel. Unfortunately for Gall, however, Columbanus was not stricken with compassion for his sick friend. Unquestioning obedience was the lifeblood of the monastery, the thing that made the monks so effective and resilient in the face of impossible adversity. There could be no excuse for disobeying Columbanus or else this small and fragile brotherhood of *peregrini pro Christo* might cease to believe in their abbot, choose easier lives, and dissolve. For this reason, Columbanus

perhaps felt the need to be harsh with Gall as a warning to the others. Before he left Gall in Bregenz, Columbanus took away his power to celebrate mass. Gall had been stripped of his supernatural power to say mass and administer the Eucharist so long as Columbanus was alive. Columbanus then gathered his monks and crossed the Alps into Italy, into the land of the Lombard king Agilulf.

The Lombards were a Germanic people that pushed into northern Italy during the sixth century. There they established a kingdom and today this particular region of Italy is known as Lombardy. When Columbanus arrived in the Kingdom of the Lombards, its people didn't share a common religion. Some were Roman Catholic, others were pagan, still others were Catholics who had broken with the pope over certain political and theological differences, and then there were a great many Christians who held unorthodox beliefs about Christ that stretched back to the days of the Roman Empire. Consequently, these differences were the source of great social unrest and instability within the kingdom.

The king and queen welcomed Columbanus and his monks with open arms because they wanted the Irishmen to promote a single religion—Roman Catholicism—among their subjects. They even hoped Columbanus might play the role of honest broker between conflicting groups. So in the year 613, they granted Columbanus the site of Bobbio, seventy miles south of Milan in the Apennine Mountains, on which to build a monastery. But Columbanus was now seventy-three years old. He simply didn't have enough years left in his life to achieve all of these things. The monastery would have to be enough. And it was. Columbanus established the monastery at Bobbio; and his disciples

eventually succeeded at turning all of Lombardy to Catholic Christianity after he was gone. Bobbio would in fact become Columbanus' most influential monastery, making vitally important gains for Irish Christianity. Sadly, Columbanus wouldn't live to see any of it.

Columbanus died at Bobbio in the year 615. Shortly before he died, he asked that his walking staff be taken into the Alps and given to his old friend Gall. So whatever became of Gall? After Columbanus left him at Bregenz, Gall climbed into a boat and rowed across Lake Constance to the house of a priest named Willimar. Gall told his friend what had happened, how he fell ill and was rebuked by his holy father Columbanus. Willimar took his sick friend under his care and appointed two clerics to nurse him back to health. When Gall was well again, he set out from Lake Constance with a deacon named Hiltibod to live alone in the mountains. They followed the River Steinach from the lake to a site between Lake Constance and the Appenzell Alps. There he established a monastery, around which grew the town of St. Gallen and the Swiss canton of the same name. The abbey that stands there today is a UNESCO World Heritage Site. Shortly after Columbanus died in 615, a monk arrived at the abbey and handed Gall Columbanus' walking staff. Gall knew what it meant. For the first time in years, St. Gall said mass and prayed for the soul of his brother in Christ, Columbanus, with whom he had set out from the shores of Ireland all those years ago in their little boat. Then, as though alone in the vast expanse of space and time, he fell to his knees and wept.

The Columbanian monasteries and the penitentials didn't fully earn their place in Catholic Europe until more than a decade after Columbanus' death. It all started in 626 when the bishops of Burgundy almost shut down the great monastery at Luxeuil for allegedly teaching false doctrine, which is to say for teaching the Irish Easter and tonsure. After narrowly averting disaster in Burgundy, the monks were determined to see that it never happened again. So in 628, the abbot of Bobbio traveled to Rome with Columbanus' hagiographer Jonas to petition the pope for a final ruling on the Irish Easter and tonsure. He was seeking a decision on the Irish Easter and tonsure that Columbanus himself was never able to get. But fortunately for the Irish, times had changed. The abbot of Bobbio was about to make tremendous gains for Irish Christianity and the monasteries.

The incident in Burgundy spurred two major developments that firmly established the Columbanian monastery as a stand-alone institution within the Roman Catholic Church. First, the pope ruled that the Columbanian monasteries were answerable directly to Rome instead of the local bishops. Prior to this decision, bishops on the continent merely assumed they had authority over the monasteries within their dioceses, as did Rome. But Pope Honorius I was a fan of the monks, particularly of their missionary work, and so he answered the abbot's plea for support by granting Bobbio and its sister monasteries freedom from episcopal control. It was a momentous decision. Never again could the bishops threaten to shutter a Columbanian monastery over the Irish Easter and tonsure. The monks were now free to spread their uniquely Irish brand of Christianity throughout Western Europe without fear of persecution from within the Church. In return for this freedom,

the pope urged the Irish to conform to the Roman Easter, to which the monasteries on the continent and the churches in southern Ireland complied by about 632. And by 716, all of Ireland had complied.

The second major development was the adoption of the Benedictine Rule. The adoption of the one rule made monasticism in the West look like a unified institution, separate and autonomous from the jurisdiction of the bishops, instead of as a host of independent houses. In this way, monasticism in Western Europe became a formidable institution alongside the diocesan churches. Columbanus had prescribed a very harsh way of life with his rule, a way of life that might have driven many men away from the monastic life. In contrast, the Benedictine Rule was easier to live by and therefore better for retaining monks. The Benedictine Rule was an obvious improvement to monastic life and was adopted widely by the Columbanian monasteries.

With the position of the monasteries assured, Irish Christianity spread rapidly throughout Western Europe. In the decades following Columbanus' death, its greatest gains were made under King Dagobert I. King Dagobert I inherited the entire Kingdom of the Franks (Neustria, Austrasia, and Burgundy) from his father Chlothar II and ruled it from 629 until his death in 639. Although Dagobert was himself devoutly religious, it was his chief counselor Eligius who was the real champion of Columbanian monasticism in Dagobert's kingdom. Because of Eligius, Dagobert's reign saw the rapid expansion of Columbanian monasteries throughout the Kingdom of the Franks.

Eligius was born near the present-day city of Cadillac, in the Bordeaux region of France, around the time Columbanus

first arrived on the Continent in 590. As a young man, he won a place at the court of King Chlothar II due to his uncommon skill as a goldsmith; and there he quickly gained a reputation for Christian piety and honesty. His reputation for honesty was so great that people would give him their gold to make jewelry without first weighing it. When Dagobert became king of Francia upon his father's death, he made Eligius his chief counselor. Eligius' reputation for piety only grew as he used his tremendous influence to promote Christian charity and to support monasteries and churches. While the details of Eligius' education are largely unknown, he must have spent time in a Columbanian monastery somewhere along the way because he was known to live by the Columbanian Rule at court. Moreover, he introduced the rule to a monastery he founded around the year 632. He also oversaw the founding of many churches throughout Francia like the *Basilique Saint-Denis*, which would go on to administer the penitentials to even greater numbers of people. For its part, the *Basilique Saint-Denis* in Paris is the burial place of nearly all French monarchs and the site of Europe's first gothic cathedral. After King Dagobert died in 639, Eligius was ordained a priest. Eventually, he was made bishop of Noyon, which is located about sixty miles north of Paris. And from Noyon, he launched missions to bring the gospel and the penitentials to the pagans of Flanders. To this day, St. Eligius is especially venerated there. St. Eligius died and was buried in Noyon in the year 660.

Within a half-century after Columbanus' death, more than a hundred monasteries were established throughout Western Europe by his disciples and by the disciples of his disciples. They founded monasteries at St. Valéry, Moutiers-Grandval, Besançon, Jouet, Altivillers, Nevers, Jumièges, Novimoutier,

St. Quentin, Charenton, Jussamoutier, Cusance, and Meaux. And they were bishops of Verdun, Vermandois, Thérouanne, Rouen, Laon, Meux, and Noyon. At least twelve monasteries were founded in Germany, all related directly or indirectly to the monastery of St. Gall. Even the English were evangelized by Columbanian monks. The English were getting Irish Christianity from all sides, from Columba's monks to the north in Britain and from Columbanus' monks to the east in continental Europe. Felix of Burgundy, a monk who was trained at a Columbanian monastery on the continent, evangelized the Kingdom of East Anglia from 630 until his death in 647. Today, he is known as St. Felix of Dunwich, apostle to the East Anglians. For a period of history that has been written off as the Dark Ages, there certainly was a lot happening.

In the year 751, after the explosion of Irish missionary activity in Western Europe, what had started as a religious calling was about to become a cultural phenomenon. For it was in 751 that a court official named Pepin the Short overthrew the Merovingian dynasty in a palace coup, thus ushering in the Carolingian period. The pope happily recognized Pepin as king of the Franks and, by papal decree, made the Carolingian name royal in law. This meant that God recognized Pepin as a king and, by virtue of Pepin's army, everyone else had better do the same. And in gratitude for the pope's support, Pepin used his powerful army to push the Lombards out of Rome's territories, leading to the creation of the Papal States. The Papal States were territories in northern Italy and southern France which were ruled by the Holy See. They existed from around this period until 1870, when the modern nation of Italy was formed. The Roman Catholic Church had struggled for centuries to establish its independence against Roman emperors, Gothic kings,

Byzantine emperors, and Lombard kings. These rulers had long sought to make the Church a vassal of their empires or kingdoms. However, with the creation of the Papal States, the Church finally achieved the political sovereignty it needed to fulfill what it saw as its mission as the universal Church to all nations. But it was Pepin's son who, of all the Carolingians, did the most to elevate Europe's great monastic movement to new heights. His name in English is Charles the Great, but we know him better by his Latin name—Charlemagne.

Charlemagne's vision for Western Europe can be described in four words: one king, one culture. To that end, he united nearly all of Western Europe under the banner of the Holy Roman Empire. Charlemagne was crowned emperor of the Romans by Pope Leo III on Christmas Day in the year 800. But Pope Leo wasn't being merely beneficent in bestowing such a lofty title upon Charlemagne. The pope owed him an incalculable debt. Pepin had given the Church the Papal States and freed it from control by the Lombards and Byzantines. And when the Lombard king Desiderius tried to regain the lands his tribe had lost to Pepin by invading the Papal States in 772, Charlemagne defeated the Lombards once and for all and assumed dominion over their lands. By defeating the Lombards and restoring the Papal States, Charlemagne put a down payment on the sovereignty of the Roman Catholic Church that would last to this day. But even more than this, Charlemagne established Roman Catholicism, and Irish Christianity in particular, as the dominant faith and culture of Western Europe through his unprecedented support for the Irish monasteries and monastic education.

Charlemagne's support for the monasteries and the schools transformed Europe. The schools were the hub of European

intellectual and cultural development throughout the Middle Ages. By the time Charlemagne was crowned sole ruler and king of the Franks in 771 at the age of twenty-nine, the monastic schools had given birth to the cathedral schools and the palace schools, which prepared the children of the nobility for careers in the Church and at the Royal Court. Quite simply, the nobility wanted bigger and better schools closer to home. Later, in the twelfth and thirteenth centuries, these cathedral schools and palace schools spawned Europe's great universities at places like Bologna, Paris, and Oxford. Yet the leap from monastic schools to universities, indeed the very establishment of education as an institution of European civilization, wouldn't have happened without Charlemagne's expansion of the schools and his educational reforms. Ironically, considering Charlemagne's insatiable appetite for learning and scholarship as an adult, he had been illiterate as a boy. Perhaps this was why he was such a great champion of the schools.

The blueprint for the new Europe was Charlemagne's crowning law the *Admonitio generalis* or General Admonition. Issued by Charlemagne in 789, its ecclesiastical and educational reforms were the legacy of Irish monasticism. Its ecclesiastical reforms imposed monastic discipline across the board by establishing guidelines for the governance of churches and the conduct of bishops and priests. At the same time, it reformed the school curriculum according to monastic practice. Charlemagne's palace was at Aachen, which today is the westernmost city in Germany; and Charlemagne endeavored to make his palace school at Aachen the best school in Europe. To this end, he recruited the best minds in Europe to make his palace school the model for all others in his empire; and perhaps the best of the best at that time was a Northumbrian clergyman

named Alcuin. Alcuin was from Britain, an Englishman who had benefited from the educational legacy of Columba and his successors at Iona and Lindisfarne. In 782, Charlemagne made Alcuin master of the palace school. Alcuin replaced the school's curriculum of military tactics and manners with the classical division of the seven liberal arts: grammar, rhetoric, dialectic, music, arithmetic, geometry, and astronomy, in addition to theology and religious training. And in 789, Charlemagne's *Admonitio generalis* made Alcuin's curriculum standard for all monastic and cathedral schools throughout the empire. But perhaps the most revolutionary educational reform of the *Admonitio generalis* was universal education. Charlemagne endeavored to educate all of his male subjects by opening existing schools to peasant boys and by requiring the construction of new schools. This was the immediate driving force behind the massive expansion of education throughout Western Europe during his reign.

The other document by which Charlemagne made education a priority in Western Europe was a letter known as the *Epistola de litteris colendis* or *Letter on the Cultivation of Learning*. The *Epistola de litteris colendis* was a letter from Charlemagne to Abbot Baugaulf at the monastery of Fulda. It was probably issued sometime during the 790s, but it could have been composed as early as 785. In it, Charlemagne directed the bishoprics and the monasteries to make education a priority of the Church. He then ordered the abbot to disseminate the letter to all of the bishops and abbots in the realm, thus making education a primary mission of the clergy in Western Europe. Charlemagne's push toward a kind of universal education was unprecedented in human history. No ruler had made education available to so many before Charlemagne.

Yet why settle only for Irish learning when you can have real Irishmen too? Accordingly, the Carolingian period saw Irishmen going to the continent in larger numbers, greatly outnumbering other contingents of foreigners at the Royal Court. It was also during this time that a kind of writing developed called Carolingian miniscule, which became the standard script throughout the Holy Roman Empire. Carolingian miniscule was derived from the way Irish scribes wrote Latin, and it later formed the basis for our modern usage of uppercase and lowercase letters. The ancient Romans wrote using only the modern equivalent of uppercase letters, which still can be seen in their inscriptions on their public buildings. But Carolingian miniscule wasn't just pretty to look at. Latin was the language of government, the Church, learning, and prosperity. By providing a uniform way to write the language, Irish scribes greatly contributed to the rise of a single European identity. Some of the more notable Irish scholars who journeyed to the continent during the Carolingian period included Clement the Irishman, Sedulius Scottus, Dicuil, Cruindmelus, Donatus of Fiesole, Dunchad of Reims, and Martinus Hibernensis. But of all the Irishmen who came to the continent during this period, the greatest was John Scotus Eriugena. He was, without a doubt, the smartest man in Europe.

John Scotus Eriugena came out of Ireland in the middle of the ninth century to become the greatest intellect of his age. He was so smart, in fact, that he was recognized as the greatest mind of his age even during his lifetime. Sadly, too little is known of his life. We don't even know his real name. Scotus merely means

Irish and Eriugena—which is a name he gave to himself—means the Irish born. He was born around the year 800. Later, in the 840s, he fled Ireland for the European mainland, probably to escape the Viking raids that plagued Ireland and Britain at the time. He probably was a monk, but he could have been a layman as well. But whether a layman or a monk, an educated man like John was a valuable thing in medieval Europe. Hence he had no problem finding a job at the Frankish Royal Court. By the year 850, he was master of the palace school at the court of King Charles the Bald. Charles was the king of Neustria and the grandson of Charlemagne. John was a shoe-in for the job of master of the palace school. He was uncommonly fluent in Greek and this alone put him head and shoulders above his peers. John also had an uncommon habit of speaking frankly with the nobility and he excelled at offending the Church. Fortunately for John, his value as a scholar probably saved him from being thrown to the wolves for his insolence.

John first drew the ire of the Church when he was asked by the archbishop of Reims and the bishop of Laon to refute a heresy. The subject was predestination, an idea first developed by Augustine that addresses the question if God knows the future, then is a person's salvation already decided before he or she is even born? Augustine said yes it is, that each person's ticket for heaven or hell is punched at birth. Pelagius, on the other hand, said no it isn't because people have free will to choose good or evil. Well it seems that a certain priest named Gottschalk had written a treatise on predestination and was imprisoned in the abbey of Hautvillers because of it. Gottschalk made the mistake of arguing that God predestines people to heaven *and* hell. This was heresy because, the Church held, God is the author of only good and never evil. Men do evil by

turning away from God, which is to say the gates of hell are locked from the inside. Gottschalk's logic was incorrigible, so the bishops drafted the best mind they could find to refute the heresy. Naturally, this meant they drafted John.

Now John wasn't necessarily looking for trouble. However, he chose to respond to Gottschalk by refuting the existence of predestination entirely; and in so doing, the bishops believed he crossed into Pelagian territory. In the eyes of the Church, John had refuted one heresy with an even worse heresy. And if that wasn't bad enough, he also was well on his way to refuting the very existence of heaven and hell! John's name was vilified by the bishops of Francia, who tried to peg him as a Pelagian for his views on free will, and he was summoned to Rome to explain himself. But Charles the Bald, not wanting to lose his prized scholar and master of his palace school, refused to give him up to the pope. It didn't hurt either that the king enjoyed John's company. One night while the two were drinking, the king asked John, "What is the difference between a drunk and an Irishman?" John leaned into the table, across from the king, and shot back, "The width of this table."

But the reason why we are still talking about John today has nothing to do with his thoughts on predestination or his renown as the king's drinking buddy. John is important because he gave Christian Europe its first new model of the cosmos since Augustine. And as time would tell, this would prove to be a crucial step toward the development of our modern worldview. Augustine had described a spiritual universe and a physical universe that were entirely separate. But John combined them into a single image that was utterly simple. It was a single circle. God and Augustine's highest heaven were at the center of the circle, while our universe was at its circumference.

John's program was part philosophy, part religion, and part mystical experience. John famously wrote, "No one enters heaven but through philosophy." Accordingly, John created his model of the cosmos by combining philosophy with religion. In technical, philosophical language, John made heavy use of three ideas from Greek philosophy called *theosis, theophany,* and *procession and return.* But in layman's terms, John created his new model of the cosmos by adding a new dimension to monastic life.

John showed the monks a new way to copy Christ. Up until this time, the Irish monks lived by the example of Christ. It was straightforward enough. They prayed, fasted, did penance, tended to the sick, labored in workshops and fields, built churches and schools, and evangelized foreign lands all in the name of living as Christ lived. But now John would do something quite different. He would show his brethren how to imitate Christ by turning inward to the world of ideas.

John wasn't happy simply acting like Christ. He wanted to think like Christ too. He wanted to participate in God's eternal being through Christ. So John developed a way to do that. He reasoned that Christ turns the mind of man away from the world of temporal things to the realm of the eternal, which ever since the time of Plato meant the world of ideas. John then developed a theology that took him from material things, then inward to the world of ideas, and finally to the idea of God. And lastly, he created his model of the cosmos to describe the experience—a single circle having God and Augustine's highest heaven at its center and our physical universe at its circumference. He intended for the believer to follow his model like a map, from our world of space and time to the realm of God eternal.

John died sometime after the year 870, probably in Britain or France. However, his model of the cosmos and his practice of following Christ inward to the realm of ideas lived on. Indeed, these became the pillars of a great intellectual movement that swept across Europe known as Scholasticism, so called because it started in the schools. John's ideas were integrated into the school curriculum largely through the work of a Burgundian monk named Remigius of Auxerre. Remigius expended great effort producing the medieval version of textbooks for his students. They were mainly compilations of classical Greek and Latin texts with commentary. But for his commentary, Remigius drew heavily upon the work of the Irish monks, particularly that of John Scotus Eriugena. Remigius died in 908, but his textbooks became standard fare in the schools.

Remigius' books were so influential that John Scotus Eriugena's practice of following Christ inward to the realm of ideas can be seen some two hundred years later in the work of St. Anselm. Anselm was a Burgundian monk who went on to become the archbishop of Canterbury in England. He was the next truly remarkable scholastic thinker after John Scotus Eriugena. In his 1078 treatise entitled *Proslogion* or *Discourse on the Existence of God*, Anselm wrote, "Enter the inner chamber of your mind; shut out all thoughts save that of God, and such as can aid you in seeking him; close your door and seek him." And it wasn't just Anselm who was following Christ into the realm of ideas. Almost every scholar in the monastery was doing it. It was so pervasive that eventually John Scotus Eriugena's cosmology became enshrined in architecture.

In the twelfth century, Abbot Suger of the *Basilique Saint-Denis* in Paris undertook to build the world's first gothic cathedral. Inspired by John Scotus Eriugena's synthesis of Augustine and the Greek theologian Pseudo-Dionysius, as well as John's translations of Pseudo-Dionysius, Abbot Suger made the interior of his cathedral a representation of infinite space and light. With its high walls, high windows, and high arches shooting into space, it was as close as any man on earth could come to Augustine's highest heaven. Then Abbot Suger did something that was in many ways even more extraordinary. He placed a model of the cosmos above the west entrance to his cathedral in the form of a round, stained glass window. Soon gothic cathedrals began appearing all over Europe. And as the cathedrals became increasingly popular, so did these windows, which came to be called rose windows.

Today, these rose windows can be seen above the entrances to cathedrals and churches the world over, but some of the most impressive are still in France at the cathedrals of Chartres and Notre Dame. These rose windows often depict religious themes like the Last Judgment or the Beatific Vision. Additionally, they are often arranged according to principles of numerology, particularly the number eight which symbolizes the eternal. But beneath all of this, they are fundamentally arranged according to the unique, Christian-Platonic cosmology that was first introduced by John Scotus Eriugena and refined by St. Anselm and his successors. God or Christ or the Blessed Virgin is usually at the center of the window; and all of creation—the spiritual universe, the celestial hierarchy of angels, and the physical universe—proceeds from and returns to the center. Importantly, these rose windows and the cathedrals they adorned helped to popularize the new cosmology among non-clergy. In time, not only would priests and monks think of God as the center of the cosmos, but so would kings and commoners as well. Hence the new cosmology became the prevailing model of the cosmos in Western Europe.

By the end of the ninth century, years of Viking raids and tribal infighting had ended the flow of Irish missionaries to the continent. Yet the Irish monks had achieved success beyond their wildest dreams. Their special kind of Irish Christianity had gone mainstream. At the Fourth Lateran Council in 1215, Rome decreed that every Christian must receive the sacrament of penance at least once a year. Irish Christianity—that form of orthodox Christianity characterized by penance, free will, and the imitation of Christ—had indeed become fully integrated into Roman Catholicism. From their humble beginnings as pilgrims for Christ to the breakthrough philosophy of John Scotus Eriugena, the Irish monks invaded Europe not with the horse and the sword, but with sandals and faith. Their work had completely transformed the continent and ushered the West into a new world. But the best was yet to come. Soon Irish Christianity would reach untold heights in the mind of a "dumb ox."

CHAPTER FIVE

Irish Christianity and the Three Wise Men

On *April 12*, 1204, the Christian knights of the Fourth Crusade crashed through the city gates of Constantinople. For three days the Crusaders pillaged and plundered the palaces and churches and homes of the great Byzantine capital. They looted sacred relics and stole priceless works of art. They looted marble and gold from the altars of churches. They stole an ancient statue of Hercules, which had been made by the sculptor Lysippus during the reign of Alexander the Great more than a thousand years earlier, and they melted it merely for its bronze. In three days, they destroyed the city's magnificent library, which had taken centuries to build. They put a whore on the bishop's seat in the Church of Hagia Sophia, the most resplendent church in all of Christendom, and made her sing for their amusement. They murdered priests and they raped nuns. They went berserk. Even the Visigoths had been more civilized when they sacked Rome in 410.

The Crusaders didn't start out with the intention of sacking the greatest city in the Christian world. The knights of the Fourth Crusade sacked Constantinople because they needed the money. They were broke and stranded on an island in the lagoon of Venice and they needed money in order to invade Muslim Egypt. Then a deposed Byzantine prince offered to give them all the money they needed for their crusade if they would use their army to restore his father as emperor. So having few options, the desperate Crusaders agreed; and under the pretense of restoring the rightful Byzantine emperor to his throne, they sacked the empire's capital city. The Crusaders never went on to fight in Egypt or any other Islamic land. The Fourth Crusade merely initiated the slow decline of the Byzantine Empire until it finally fell to the Ottoman Turks in 1453; and today Constantinople is called Istanbul. Yet if there was one saving grace to the whole disastrous affair, then it was Aristotle.

In the course of sacking Constantinople, the Crusaders seized upon certain works of Aristotle in their original Greek and carried them back to Western Europe. Aristotle's books on logic were never lost to the West, but most of his books including those on natural philosophy, metaphysics, and the soul had gone missing since the fall of Rome. Christian Europe rediscovered those books when the Moorish stronghold of Toledo, Spain fell to King Alfonso VI of Castile in the year 1085. But the books they found in Toledo were written in Arabic and riddled with ideas that were falsely attributed to Aristotle. So the Europeans made Latin translations from inaccurate Arabic translations of the original Greek versions, which the Moors no longer seemed to possess. Now with the rediscovery of the original Greek versions, Europeans would finally have the opportunity to see what Aristotle really said about God, man, and nature. And for a brilliant Dominican friar named Thomas Aquinas, Aristotle would provide the challenge he needed to become one of the greatest thinkers the world has ever known.

Thomas Aquinas was born in the year 1225 at his family's castle in Roccasecca, a town in the Italian province of Frosinone south of Rome. The earth beneath the town has known both the thundering march of Roman legions heading into battle and the humble sandals of monks following in the footsteps of Christ. During World War II, the town was held by Hitler until the Allies came and bombed the Nazis back to Berlin. In that battle, many of the townspeople paid for freedom with their lives. But in all its centuries of hosting human history, the town of Roccasecca has become most famous as the birthplace of St. Thomas Aquinas.

Thomas was born of nobility. His family tree was indeed overgrown with noble relatives that included Holy Roman Emperors Henry VI and Frederick II, and the kings of Castile, Aragon, and France. The town of Aquino, situated just six miles to the south of Roccasecca, was the seat of his family's power and the origin of the name Aquinas. And eight miles to the east of Aquino was the renowned Benedictine monastery of Monte Cassino, where Thomas' uncle served as abbot. Abbot of Monte Cassino was a very prestigious position within the Roman Catholic Church. Monte Cassino was the most prominent monastery in all of Europe, founded in the year 529 by St. Benedict himself. It was famous as the place where Benedict wrote his rule for administering monasteries and governing the lives of monks, a rule which endures to this day. The original Abbey of Monte Cassino, however, wasn't so lucky. Tragically, the American army destroyed it in 1944 when an intelligence report said there were more Germans in the monastery than monks. It has since been rebuilt.

Although Thomas was born of nobility, he would never inherit his father's title or estates. That honor was reserved for first-born sons. Unfortunately for little Tomasso, he was the fourth son of Count Landulf of Aquino and Countess Theodora of Teano. The count and countess knew, however, that wealth and power might also be obtained through the Church. After all, Thomas' uncle had control over considerable Church lands and a direct line of communication to the pope as the abbot of Monte Cassino. So in the year 1230, when Thomas was about five years old, Landulf and Theodora sent Thomas as an oblate to Monte Cassino where they hoped he would one day succeed his uncle as abbot of the most celebrated monastery in Europe.

At the monastery, Thomas was educated according to the standard curriculum of his time: first the trivium of grammar, rhetoric, and dialectic; and then the quadrivium of music, arithmetic, geometry, and astronomy. This was the classical division of the seven liberal arts, which had been the standard curriculum in Europe's schools since the reign of Charlemagne. Legend has it that little Tomasso was a taciturn student, speaking only to ask, "What is God?" The question prefigured what Thomas Aquinas would later write as a man: "Contemplation of the divine truth is the end of the whole human life." But most of all, Thomas' education from childhood into adulthood was dominated by the intellectual movement known as Scholasticism.

Scholasticism had its origin in the teachings of the Irishman John Scotus Eriugena; and it was founded on his basic explanation for how Christ actually brings men to God. To imitate Christ meant to think like Christ; and to think like Christ meant to know the realm of the eternal. So the Scholastics believed that Christ led the mind inward to the realm of the eternal, which for John Scotus Eriugena was the realm of ideas. It was a concept that John and the Scholastics had on good authority from Augustine and the Platonists.

According to Augustine, ideas were eternal because they came from the eternal mind of God. Ideas were the building blocks of God's creation. Just as the guitar maker has an idea of the guitar in his mind before he creates it, so too does God have an idea of each thing he creates. For this reason, Augustine, the Platonists, and the Scholastics all believed that ideas were more real and enduring than material things. Therefore, the Scholastics concluded, the contemplation of ideas ultimately brought men closer to God. The greater the idea, they thought, the closer one was to the Creator.

This was why the Scholastics needed schools, because they sought to go from Christ to the realm of ideas to God through learning and scholarship. Indeed, Scholasticism was so named because it started in the schools. For the Scholastics, doing philosophy and theology was how they indirectly contemplated the divine truth in this life. Schools were vitally important to them for getting nearer to God. As for the next life, Thomas wrote, "...we shall see God face to face, wherefore it will make us perfectly happy." In light of the dominance of Scholasticism during the High and Late Middle Ages, it's no wonder why this period of European history witnessed the invention of the university.

Thomas spent nine years at Monte Cassino before leaving at the age of fourteen to continue his education at the newly founded University of Naples. Universities were new to Europe in the thirteenth century, an outgrowth of the palace schools and the cathedral schools which had been established by clergy under the patronage of kings. Europe's first universities were the University of Paris and the University of Bologna,

both founded in 1200. Oxford was founded shortly thereafter in 1210 and the rest followed. When Thomas left Monte
Cassino in 1239, the University of Naples was just fifteen years
old, founded in 1224 by Thomas' second cousin Holy Roman
Emperor Frederick II. The young university was the perfect
place for Thomas' fecund mind. At the University of Naples,
Thomas continued his education in the liberal arts under the
tutelage of Peter of Ireland. It was here that Peter of Ireland
introduced Thomas to certain works of Aristotle beyond those
already included in the liberal arts curriculum. Thomas also
studied Christian-Platonist authors like Augustine, Boethius,
and Pseudo-Dionysius and he studied Neoplatonist authors like
Proclus, all of which gave him a firm grounding in Platonism.
In 1244, Thomas left Naples to continue his education at the
University of Paris. But something was about to go awry in
the life of the young saint. He would not arrive at Paris as
planned. Unbeknownst to Thomas, he would soon be kid-
napped, imprisoned in a castle for a year, and tempted by a
prostitute to abandon the path of Christ.

At the dawn of the thirteenth century, two new religious
orders were born in Europe. They were the Franciscans and
the Dominicans. St. Francis of Assisi was the son of an affluent
Italian cloth merchant who rejected his family's wealth for a
life of Christian poverty. He founded the Franciscan Order
in the year 1209. In 1219, he went to Egypt to evangelize
the Muslims. There he was taken prisoner by the Saracens
and was brought before Sultan Melek-el-Kamel. And there,
before the sultan, Francis challenged his Muslim captors to a

test of faith. Francis proposed to walk through a raging bon-
fire unharmed as proof that Christ is God; and he invited the
Muslims to do the same to prove the divinity of Allah. Francis
then volunteered to go first into the flames on the condition
that if he emerged unharmed, the sultan would confess that
Christ is God. Francis' captors refused his challenge and the
sultan was never converted. Yet while Francis failed to win
the sultan's soul, he won the sultan's respect and admiration
for his indomitable faith. Before parting ways, the sultan asked
Francis, "Pray for me that God may deign to reveal to me that
law and faith which is most pleasing to him."

The other Christian revolutionary of the early thirteenth
century was a Spaniard named Dominic de Guzmán. He
founded the Dominican Order in the year 1215. As the story
goes, Dominic was on a diplomatic mission for the king of
Castile when he encountered the Cathars in southern France.
The Cathars, who were also called Albigensians, were the thirteenth-century incarnation of the Manichees. They preached
primarily in southern France, in the Languedoc region, and
had attracted quite a large following by the time St. Dominic
first encountered them around the year 1203. Dominic was
so alarmed by the pervasiveness of the Manichean heresy in
southern France that he formed the Dominican Order to teach
correct doctrine to the masses of people who had been mislead
by the Cathars.

Both the Franciscans and the Dominicans were revolutionary because they were radically evangelical. That is to say, they
journeyed out of the monasteries and into the cities and towns
in order to minister to the people, taking a vow of poverty and
relying solely on charity for their support. Such a thing had
never been done before by a Catholic religious order. They

were so dedicated to living a poor and pious life that they eventually came to be known as mendicant friars. Yet despite their poverty, the mendicant friars were highly educated men. The Dominicans in particular placed special emphasis on learning and scholarship, which Dominic believed was necessary in order to show the people the truth of Catholicism and the error of the Cathars. For an introspective young nobleman named Thomas Aquinas, this total dedication to God through the contemplative life drew him to the Dominican Order like a moth to a flame.

Thomas' father died at the end of 1243. Less than a year later in 1244, Thomas joined the Dominican Order while still a student at the University of Naples. His father's death must have played a considerable role in Thomas' decision to join the Dominicans. With his father gone, perhaps Thomas felt there was no longer anyone or anything stopping him from striking out on his own; or perhaps the life hereafter suddenly seemed more real to Thomas than our short lives here on earth; or perhaps both. On the other hand, Thomas' mother was furious. To Theodora, her son was diminishing the family's power and influence by throwing away a very promising future as abbot of Monte Cassino. In her mind, if she was going to save the family from her son's colossal lapse of judgment, then desperate times would require desperate measures.

Thomas' family did what any family might do in a similar situation—they staged the medieval version of an intervention. Thomas' brothers seized him on the road to Paris and brought him to the family castle at Roccasecca, where they locked him in a room. Thomas' brothers sent a prostitute to his room hoping the desires of the flesh might conquer the will of his spirit. But Thomas would have none of it. When the woman entered his room, Thomas rose to his feet and seized a piece of burning wood from the fireplace. In defense of his virtue, he drove the woman from his room with the firebrand and slammed the door shut. Then he burned the sign of the cross into the wooden door as protection from further temptation. Thomas prayed to God for deliverance from evil and fell into a deep sleep. As the story goes, that night two angels came to him in a dream bearing God's blessing of a life free from carnal desire; and by the grace of God, Thomas would never be aggrieved by lust again. To the devout, medieval audiences that first heard these stories of the saint's life, Thomas' deliverance from the disobedience of the flesh was proof of God's divine mercy.

While divine intervention may have freed Thomas from the bonds of lust, it was the intervention of a more earthly power which freed Thomas from the family ties that bound him to Roccasecca. Ultimately, Thomas was forced to appeal to the pope for his release from the family castle. Luckily for Thomas, Pope Innocent IV was a big fan of the Franciscans and the Dominicans. In their unique role as monks among the people, the Franciscans and Dominicans had become the foot soldiers of Catholic orthodoxy against heretics like the Cathars. So relentless were these new orders in combating heresy that on April 20, 1233, Pope Gregory IX put the Dominicans in charge of the Inquisition. It was a role by which the Dominican Order earned the moniker *Domini canes* or the hounds of heaven. And a grateful Pope Gregory returned the favor by freeing Thomas from the family castle in order to continue his education at the University of Paris as a Dominican friar.

Thomas studied at the University of Paris from 1245 to 1248 under Albertus Magnus, a name which translates from

Latin as Albert the Great. Albert was an eminent Dominican friar and German theologian who possessed a keen understanding of Aristotle's philosophy. Today he is known for having been one of the greatest scholastic philosophers as well as the teacher of Thomas Aquinas. Thomas, on the other hand, was tall and corpulent and quiet, a combination of silence and size that led some of his classmates to derisively call him a "dumb ox." We might call Thomas heavy set, chubby, or even fat. Yet where others saw a taciturn oaf, Albert saw brilliance. Albert reproached the others by telling them, "We call this young man a dumb ox, but so loud will be his bellowing in doctrine that it will resound throughout the world." Albert couldn't have known just how right he was.

Albert and Thomas left Paris for the German city of Cologne in 1248, where Albert headed the new university there. Meanwhile, Thomas continued his lengthy education. He studied theology and Aristotle, wrote scholarly works, assisted Albert with teaching, and was ordained a priest. It was a very productive time for him. Then in 1252, Thomas returned to the University of Paris to complete his education for the degree of master of theology, which was the highest degree the university could bestow. The master of theology degree was a kind of thirteenth-century Ph.D. It was such a monumental undertaking that it took Thomas four more years of full-time study to earn the degree. But sure enough in 1256, Thomas was named master of theology. In the wake of his well-earned success, Thomas was appointed to the Dominican's chair on the faculty of the University of Paris. Nothing it seemed could stop Thomas Aquinas now. Nothing, that is, except a large contingent of faculty who refused to recognize his membership in their club. Thomas, it seems, had become the unwitting victim of a long-standing feud between the secular clergy and the mendicant friars.

Secular clergy are those clergy within the Catholic Church who don't belong to a religious order. They're called secular clergy because they live in cities or towns (as opposed to monasteries) and owe their obedience to a bishop instead of an abbot. Examples include deacons and priests attached to diocesan churches. In the thirteenth century, the secular clergy clashed with the newly formed Dominican and Franciscan Orders over matters both political and religious. To the secular clergy, the evangelical Dominicans and Franciscans descended upon a city or town to steal souls and take offerings that might have otherwise gone to the local church; and all of this without so much as a nod to the local priest. They believed the Dominicans and Franciscans belonged in monasteries, not among the people in cities and towns. To put it mildly, the bishops and priests greatly resented the competition from the friars.

The main battleground for this conflict between the secular clergy and the newly formed Franciscan and Dominican Orders was the University of Paris. At the time, it was the most prestigious center of learning in all of Europe. And as an institution founded by the Church, everyone on the faculty was a member of the clergy. Consequently, divisions within the faculty developed along religious lines. The Dominicans and Franciscans formed their own tight-knit communities and worked vigorously to secure positions within the university. Not surprisingly, it didn't take long before their detractors began to accuse them of colluding to bestow degrees upon each other and advance their own to coveted faculty positions. This alone made them plenty of enemies. But the bad blood between the secular priests and the mendicant friars boiled over in 1229 when the Dominicans and Franciscans refused to join the secular clergy in a strike against the local Paris government. During that crisis, the university faculty closed the school and refused to teach for two years to protest the rough treatment of its students by the local police. But the friars' failure to stand in solidarity with the secular clergy created a rift between the two that would last for decades. They crossed the picket line, so to speak. Over the next twenty years, the secular clergy and the mendicant friars maintained an uneasy peace until the feud erupted anew in 1252.

This time the charge was led by William of St. Amour, a secular priest and member of the Paris faculty. William and his contingent of secular clergy attempted to halt the friars' growing influence within the university by suspending their teaching privileges, but the friars ignored the suspension and continued teaching. Then William and his supporters petitioned Pope Innocent IV to rescind the privilege the friars enjoyed of ministering to the people without the permission of the local priest. In 1254, the pope granted the petition, partially for personal reasons. The Dominican Order had offended the pope by refusing to grant his family a coveted piece of land it owned on which to build a castle. God, it seemed, had abandoned the friars. But then they had an auspicious stroke of luck. Pope Innocent IV died in December of 1254 and was succeeded by Pope Alexander IV. And fortunately for the mendicant friars, the new pope was Cardinal Protector of the Franciscan Order. He naturally sided with the friars and repealed the actions taken against them during the reign of his predecessor. With the pope on their side, the friars appeared victorious. But William had one last trick up his sleeve.

Having lost the fight to exclude the Dominicans and Franciscans from academic and pastoral life, William wrote a scathing polemic against the friars in 1256. It was, in fact, a very clever piece of propaganda. He developed a laundry list of signs for use in identifying false apostles, which he based on the practices and behaviors of the friars. Then he accused the friars of being false apostles, and even claimed that they were preparing the way for the coming of the Antichrist. In other words, William's signs were merely a chopping block for his hatchet job. His list of signs included practicing nepotism and relying on logic and reason instead of the divine revelation of Holy Scripture. William's propaganda campaign against the friars would eventually backfire. But unfortunately for Thomas, it came just in time to delay his success.

By the time Thomas was appointed to the faculty at Paris in 1256, the bad blood between the secular clergy and the mendicant friars had been brewing there for more than twenty-five years. Nevertheless, Thomas attempted to take his place among them. The hostility was so palpable that Thomas was forced to give his inaugural lecture under the protection of an armed guard. Also that same year, Thomas and his Franciscan colleague Bonaventure wrote separate treatises to defend their orders against William of St. Amour's nasty accusations. St. Bonaventure is today regarded as one of the major thinkers of his age. Like Thomas, Bonaventure had also been appointed to the faculty in 1256 and had been blacklisted by William and his cohorts. The situation between the priests and the friars got so bad that, finally, the pope was forced to intervene on behalf of the friars. The following year in 1257, the secular clergy were compelled by order of the pope to acknowledge Thomas and Bonaventure's membership among the faculty. As for William of St. Amour, he was excommunicated by the pope, exiled from France, and his polemic against the mendicant friars was ordered burned. The situation was so heated that William was probably lucky that he wasn't burned along with his writings.

Thomas left the University of Paris in 1259 and spent the next ten years teaching in Italy. Italy was likely a welcome change for Thomas following the turmoil of Paris. During these years, Thomas held teaching posts at Naples, the town of Orvieto (which is about eighty miles north of Rome), Viterbo (which is also north of Rome), and in Rome itself at the Basilica of Santa Sabina, which has been the headquarters of the Dominican Order since the year 1219. But the scenery wasn't the only thing that changed in Thomas' life. The focus of his intellectual life also became sharper. For it was during this period that Thomas devoted himself fully to solving the major problem of his day—Aristotle. Indeed, the ten-year period from 1259 to 1268 was the most prolific of Thomas' writing career, seeing him produce most of his literary corpus. Unfortunately, he never completed his most ambitious work, the *Summa theologiae* or *Summary of Theology*, due to his untimely death in 1274 at the age of forty-eight.

When the Crusaders sacked Constantinople in 1204, they didn't merely rediscover Aristotle. They rediscovered Aristotle's complete model of the cosmos—a model of God, man, and nature that had been lost to the Christian West since the fall of Rome. Europeans had never lost Aristotle's model of the physical universe, which had been refined by the Roman astronomer Ptolemy in the second century AD. Throughout the Middle

Ages, scholars and theologians universally accepted Aristotle and Ptolemy's basic premise that the earth was at the center of the universe. But nobody was certain where Aristotle had placed God until his books on natural philosophy, metaphysics, and the soul were rediscovered in their original Greek.

Aristotle had conceived a model of the cosmos that was nearly the opposite of the one everybody in medieval Europe knew and accepted, which is to say the one that was depicted by the rose window. Aristotle placed the earth at the center of the cosmos and he placed his idea of God at its circumference. And because he was a pagan who lived more than three hundred years before Christ, he didn't account for Judeo-Christian principles such as the idea that God creates from nothing. So his explanations for how the universe works, the true nature of God, and the relationship of God to man were not only dramatically different from those of the Christian theologians who came after him, but they also contradicted many core beliefs of the Christian faith. It doesn't seem like much today, but in the thirteenth century it threatened to throw European civilization into utter chaos. Because if there's one thing no civilization can withstand, it's competing models of the cosmos.

At first, the Church tried to ban Aristotle. That didn't work. Then it tried to censor Aristotle. But that didn't work either. The Church leadership simply couldn't suppress Aristotle the way it suppressed other heresies. Scholars kept ignoring the bans and circumventing the censorship because so many learned men esteemed Aristotle's books as highly as the Bible. Indeed, this wouldn't have been such a problem had it been anyone other than Aristotle. Aristotle was so highly regarded that even Thomas Aquinas referred to him simply as

"The Philosopher." The only problem was that learned men were left wondering who to believe, the Church or Aristotle. For Christian Europe, the only thing worse might have been finding the body of Jesus in a tomb somewhere.

Hence the challenge facing Thomas was how to square Aristotle with Christianity. And since the conflicting doctrines of both Aristotle and the Church were founded on their respective cosmologies, Thomas Aquinas needed to fix the problem at the source. He needed to find a new model of the cosmos that would make Aristotle compatible with Christian doctrine. It was no mean feat. Thomas certainly had his work cut out for him. Thomas, however, understood Aristotle better than anyone. And he used his remarkable intellect to come up with an astonishingly elegant solution to the problem: he *reversed* the positions of heaven and earth in the rose-window model of the cosmos. He moved heaven to the circumference of the circle and earth to its center. And once man and God were in the same positions in both the Christian and Aristotelian models (man at the center of the circle and God at the circumference), Thomas could begin to show how most of Aristotle's core ideas were compatible with Christianity.

Perhaps surprisingly, Thomas' solution was inspired by certain ideas of the Islamic polymath Avicenna. Avicenna was an eleventh-century Persian physician, philosopher, and one of the great Islamic interpreters of Aristotle. In addition to studying the best minds of classical antiquity and Christendom, Thomas studied the works of Islamic philosophers like Avicenna, as well as those of esteemed Jewish thinkers like the great Moses Maimonides. The study of Jewish and Islamic thinkers by Christian scholars was quite common at the time. Indeed, the Late Middle Ages saw a vibrant exchange of ideas between Christians, Muslims, and Jews. At the heart of Thomas' solution was the concept of existence. In a bold move inspired by Avicenna, Thomas said that God does not have existence, but rather God is existence itself. God is not a being, but rather God is being itself. Thomas reasoned that no created thing can create itself. Created things must have their existence caused by another. But God was different. Thomas asserted that God, as the first efficient cause of everything, didn't have his existence caused by another. God has always existed. He is eternal. Therefore, according to Thomas, existence itself subsisted in God. Put another way, God is existence itself or subsistent existence. In Thomas' mind, it was the very name by which God identified himself to Moses in Exodus: "I am that I am."

Crucially, it also meant that everything in the cosmos depended on God's existence for its existence. For nothing can exist apart from existence itself any more than a painting can exist apart from its canvas. And because God is the very canvas of the cosmos, everything that exists necessarily does so in God. In philosophical language, everything that exists participates in God's existence. It was just the idea Thomas needed in order to place mankind and the entire physical universe in God. It was the idea he needed to move our world from the circumference of the cosmos to its center. Thus Thomas placed the earth, moon, sun, planets, and stars in an infinite space that he called God's existence. Thomas, for the first time in history, placed the entire physical universe in the infinite space of Augustine's highest heaven. And it would prove to be a major turning point in the development of Western civilization.

The challenge facing Thomas, however, didn't merely entail making Aristotle compatible with Christianity. He also had to defeat a solution to the problem from another group whose cure was worse than the disease. In 1268, Thomas left Rome and returned to teach at the University of Paris where he found himself in the thick of it. There he encountered Siger of Brabant, a member of the Paris faculty who championed a philosophical movement called Latin Averroism. Siger was the leader of the Averroists, a contingent of faculty members who believed that Aristotle could be made compatible with Christianity by applying the ideas of the twelfth-century Islamic philosopher Averroes. Averroes, in his attempt to make Aristotle compatible with the Koran, held that philosophy reveals literal truths whereas Scripture is merely allegorical of those same truths. In other words, he taught that philosophy trumped the Koran. He believed the literal interpretation of the Koran was meant to instruct the uneducated masses that were incapable of doing philosophy; and he cautioned Islamic theologians to keep their allegorical interpretations out of the public square to avoid confusing the common man. In the context of Christianity, the Averroists had no qualms admitting that Aristotle's philosophy and the Bible contradicted each other; hence the need to resort to allegory to reconcile the two. Yet the idea of allegorizing Scripture to make it compatible with philosophy was hardly new. John Scotus Eriugena said very much the same thing as Averroes when his philosophy began to run afoul of Church doctrine. And in the fourth century, Ambrose showed Augustine how to allegorize Scripture in order to avoid potential conflicts with the scholarship of his time. Even in the first century, the Jewish theologian Philo of Alexandria allegorized Hebrew Scripture in an effort to make Plato's philosophy compatible with Judaism. But Thomas didn't buy it. Thomas believed Aristotle could be made compatible with Scripture without resorting to allegory. Moreover, he believed that if the Averroists were allowed to prevail, philosophy would trump Christianity and men would become slaves to the ideologies of other men.

Thomas went head to head with the Averroists and directly challenged their doctrines, which he saw as diminishing the authority of the Bible. We can just see Thomas now, this ox of a man playing to a packed hall, standing to raise his voice to decry false doctrine and then lowering it again to explain to an enthralled crowd his stunning synthesis of Aristotle and Christianity. In the end, the Church sided with Thomas and he won the debate. Then, in 1270, the bishop of Paris condemned Averroism and issued a stern warning to the Paris faculty not to teach it. Meanwhile, others attacked the seeming hypocrisy of the Averroists for preaching Aristotle in the classroom while practicing Christianity in church. They made the Averroists look foolish for teaching that both Aristotle's philosophy and the Bible were true even when they seemed to contradict one another. This parody of logic came to be known as double truth and was immortalized by the Italian poet Dante Alighieri. In his *Divine Comedy*, Dante has Thomas eulogize Siger in heaven with the words,

> *This is the eternal light of Siger,*
> *who, when he lectured in the Street of Straw,*
> *proved by his syllogisms displeasing truths.*

The reference to "displeasing truths" points to the condemnation of 1277, in which the bishop of Paris ridiculed the Averroists by writing, "For they say that these things are true according to philosophy but not according to the Catholic faith, as if there were two contrary truths...." Yet if an Averroist ever said such a thing, it was merely to avoid being put on trial before the Inquisition for denying the supreme authority of Holy Scripture. Their fears were not unfounded. Siger was later condemned to death by the Inquisition, but eventually had his sentence overturned on appeal. In the end, however, Dante had the last word. He placed Siger in heaven alongside Thomas Aquinas, perhaps because he saw the same truth in the ideas of both men.

Thomas' solution to the Aristotle problem was not only elegant. It was revolutionary. In the mind's eye, Thomas made infinite space the background of each and every material thing. And this simple, esthetic change would prove to be the very foundation of our modern worldview.

Dante's *Divine Comedy* was the most dramatic sign that the Western worldview had changed. Written between 1308 and his death in 1321, the *Divine Comedy* is Dante's literary masterpiece of man's journey to God. It tells the story of Dante's trip through hell, purgatory, and heaven during Holy Week in the year 1300. In writing the *Divine Comedy*, Dante drew heavily from Thomas' theology. Indeed, the climax of the story comes when Dante finally reaches God and sees the Beatific Vision, which was the name Thomas Aquinas gave to man's contemplation of God face to face in the afterlife. But all along the way, Dante gives Western civilization Thomas Aquinas' model of the cosmos in Technicolor.

Dante's *Divine Comedy* did for Thomas Aquinas what the rose window did for John Scotus Eriugena. It popularized his cosmology. Like Augustine's *Confessions*, Dante's *Divine Comedy* was meant to be performed. It was television for the Middle Ages, read aloud to public audiences for even the most illiterate peasant to hear. It went a long way toward popularizing Thomas' model of the cosmos. Yet Thomas didn't just change the way people saw the cosmos as a whole. He offered a new way of seeing each and every material object in the cosmos.

Before Thomas Aquinas, Western thinkers understood the world largely in terms of hierarchies. Plato and Aristotle were arguably the most influential ancient philosophers. They held that the cosmos was arranged as a hierarchy of ideas or forms from the greatest of things to the least of things, from heaven to earth. Not all Greek and Roman philosophers believed in a heaven or metaphysics like Plato and Aristotle. But they still believed that the natural order of things was a hierarchy, with human beings at the top and inanimate objects like stones at the bottom. And among human beings, men were greater than women, kings were greater than commoners, and free men were greater than slaves. This idea of a natural hierarchy was why people believed some men were born to be kings while others were born to be slaves.

The way out of hierarchies was the esthetic of infinite space. If a person could conceptualize objects against the background of infinite space, then he or she could see those objects as individual things apart from any supposed natural order or hierarchy. The ancient Greek philosopher Epicurus and the Roman poet Lucretius both conceptualized the universe as an infinite void. And Augustine introduced the idea of infinite space to the Christian mind in the fifth century, thus setting the West on the path to modernity. But nobody extended it to the earthly human environment. The infinite space or void was always in outer space or in heaven, while the earth remained chock-full of material things arranged from the greatest to the least. Then Thomas Aquinas changed all of that.

Thomas Aquinas gave philosophers and theologians a way to conceptualize individual things apart from all other things, in an environment that was entirely the product of Christian theology. He gave them a way to see things in isolation, apart from their place in any supposed hierarchy. And he did so by showing philosophers and theologians how to conceptualize each and every material object against the background of God's infinite existence.

How he did it is somewhat technical. Thomas reasoned that before we can know what a thing is, we must first know that it exists. Thus human beings innately know the concept of existence from the moment they are born. It is hardwired into the human intellect. For without the ability to know whether or not a thing exists, we couldn't know anything at all. But Thomas went further. He also said that each and every material object depends on God's existence for its existence. Put another way, every material object in the universe necessarily exists upon an infinite canvas which is existence itself. For just as a painting cannot exist apart from its canvas, so too can nothing exist apart from existence itself. And this infinite canvas is God.

So in Thomas' theology, first we apprehend that an object exists. Then, having discerned that the object exists, we see it as an *individual* thing against the fabric of the infinite cosmos, which is existence itself. We see it as *one* thing apart from all other things.

Thomas' revolutionary theology gave the West an entirely new way of seeing the world. It was nothing less than an esthetic transformation of the Western mind. In terms of how human beings conceptualize material objects, it was the intellectual equivalent of taking eggs from a basket one at a time and holding them up to the sky. Thomas gave mankind a way to conceptualize individual objects in isolation, against the background of an infinite space like a single egg against a clear blue sky. The great Irish writer James Joyce described this process in his novel *A Portrait of the Artist as a Young Man* during a scene in which his protagonist, Stephen Dedalus, invokes Aquinas to expound on esthetics:

> *In order to see that basket, said Stephen, your mind first of all separates the basket from the rest of the visible universe which is not the basket. The first phase of apprehension is a bounding line drawn about the object to be apprehended. An esthetic image is presented to us either in space or in time. What is audible is presented in time, what is visible is presented in space. But, temporal or spatial, the esthetic image is first luminously apprehended as selfbounded and selfcontained upon the immeasurable background of space or time which is not it. You apprehend it as* one thing. *You see it as one whole. You apprehend its wholeness. That is* integritas.

Like a ball set on a soccer pitch, the object is automatically isolated for the observer against the background on which it sits. For Thomas Aquinas, the "bounding line drawn about the object to be apprehended" is the object's existence and the "immeasurable background of space or time" is God's existence. All the mind is doing is separating objects according to the principle that they exist and then placing them against the background of God's existence, which is an esthetic background that originated with Augustine's highest heaven. This unique mental environment then automatically isolates the object for the observer.

But where James Joyce saw infinite space, Thomas Aquinas saw God's existence. Essentially, they are two different ways of describing the fabric of the cosmos; and the difference is vast. Thomas Aquinas believed the fabric of the cosmos was God's existence. In his theology, the concept of existence was what enabled the human intellect to ascertain knowledge of both the physical world and God. And because the human intellect and every material object participated in God's existence, Thomas reasoned that men could learn certain things about God from observing objects, such as whether God exists. So he examined man and nature for what they could tell him about God. It was like examining a clock to see what it could tell about the clock maker. Yet by the time James Joyce published *A Portrait of the Artist as a Young Man* in 1916, Western scholars had abandoned this idea. They saw no connection between objects and God that might provide a window into heaven. The modern view is that objects merely provide a window into nature, an axiom which is foundational to modern science. And this idea would soon enter the Western mind in the decades following Thomas Aquinas' death. Soon two Franciscan friars would show the world the hidden power of mere empty space.

In 1272, Thomas left Paris for the last time and returned to the University of Naples to teach. Less than two years later, while saying mass on December 6, 1273, Thomas had an ecstatic vision that compelled him to declare, "I can write nothing more. Everything I have written seems like straw compared to what I have seen." Three months later he would be dead. In January 1274, the pope summoned Thomas to an ecumenical council at Lyon. He never made it. Thomas became ill en route to the council and died in Italy on March 7, 1274, at the monastery of Fossanova. Today his body is interred at the Dominican church in Toulouse, France, while his soul remains on display in the *Divine Comedy* where Dante counts him among the souls of the wise in the heaven of the sun.

Thomas was canonized by Pope John XXII at Avignon in 1323. But Thomas' road to sainthood wasn't without controversy. When the bishop of Paris condemned the Averroists in 1277, he cited 219 propositions that were said to contradict the Catholic faith, some of which were attributable to Thomas. The charges were so serious that an elderly Albertus Magnus appeared in person to defend his late student's good name. And Paris wasn't the only place where Thomas' orthodoxy was called into question. At Oxford, the archbishop of Canterbury issued condemnations that were almost identical to those issued at Paris. The controversy surrounding Thomas during these years was the culmination of a long-standing rivalry between the Franciscans and the Dominicans. For the longest time there had been bad blood brewing between the friars. The two orders had started out as siblings, equal in every respect. But over the years the Dominicans had become more powerful within the Church and the Franciscans resented it.

The Dominicans controlled the Inquisition and now, with the rising popularity of Thomas' system, they were becoming tremendously influential over doctrine as well. And so in those years following Thomas' death, in this very heated political climate that pitted brother against brother, two Franciscan friars would inadvertently unleash the potential of Thomism in their efforts to rein it in. John Duns Scotus and William of Ockham were about to unleash the modern world.

John Duns Scotus was born around the year 1266 in Ireland or Scotland and most likely was raised in a Franciscan monastery. He later joined the Franciscan Order as a friar and was ordained to the priesthood in 1291. It's unknown whether John was born rich or poor. In those days, families both rich and poor sent their sons to be educated at monasteries. And John certainly received a first-rate education. He might have formed his philosophy and his criticisms of Thomism while studying at the University of Oxford from 1288 to 1301. Of course he could just as well have formed them after leaving Oxford, while lecturing at Cambridge or Paris.

John taught at Cambridge for a brief time after leaving Oxford in 1301. But by the autumn of 1302, he had taken a job teaching at Paris only to have his career cut short by the King of France. He was expelled from Paris for allegedly taking the pope's side in a titanic dispute between the pope and the king. In 1296, King Philip IV and Pope Boniface VIII came to blows over the issue of taxing the clergy. The king began taxing the clergy without the pope's permission in order to pay for his wars with England and Flanders. And in Rome's view, taxing the clergy without the pope's permission was a grave violation of Church sovereignty.

Pope Boniface was probably right to oppose the king's tax on the clergy, but he was certainly wrong in the way he went about it. The pope should have used the incident to remind the king of the separate powers of the Church and the state and why it was important for the one to be independent of the other. He should have reminded the king that while he was ordained by

God to govern men's bodies, the Church was ordained by God to save their souls; and that taxing the clergy was the same as taxing Christ himself. He should have reminded the king that the Church was the living Body of Christ on earth; and that a king who taxed the King of kings defied the divine order. In short, he should have advanced a narrow interpretation of the doctrine of the Two Powers, which Pope Gelasius I articulated in 494. In making these arguments, the pope would have had a better chance at reaching a diplomatic solution to the problem instead of inviting confrontation. But, ultimately, Pope Boniface botched the affair and made his argument against the king exactly backwards.

Instead of arguing that the king had no power over the Church, Pope Boniface argued that the Church had unmitigated power over the king. Instead of telling the king that he lacked the authority to tax clergy, the pope told him that he had to obey Rome's order to stop. In his infamous bull *Unam sanctam* or *The One Holy*, Pope Boniface wrote, "However, one sword ought to be subordinated to the other and temporal authority, subjected to spiritual power." But that wasn't the worst part. He ended the bull with the incendiary line, "Furthermore, we declare, we proclaim, we define that it is absolutely necessary for salvation that every human creature be subject to the Roman Pontiff."

Not surprisingly, the bull went over with King Philip like a lead balloon. Pope Boniface issued the bull on November 18, 1302; and by the following year, King Philip was expelling every suspected papist from Paris, including John Duns Scotus and a majority of his Franciscan brothers. Then in September of 1303, King Philip's henchmen got a hold of Pope Boniface at his palace in Anagni, Italy, where they beat the tar out of him and threw the old man in prison for two days without food or water. They nearly killed him. He was finally freed by the townspeople on the third day. Boniface died at Rome about a month later, probably as a result of the beating.

Following the death of Pope Boniface, tensions between King Philip and the Church cooled enough to allow John to return to Paris. John's year in exile, which he spent teaching at Oxford, was finally over. John was named Franciscan regent master of theology at Paris in 1304, which was the medieval equivalent of getting tenure at the most prestigious university in the world. He held that chair until 1307, when he was transferred by the Franciscan Order from Paris to the university at Cologne. It was the last time he would ever see Paris. John Duns Scotus died at Cologne in 1308 at the age of forty-two. Fortunately, John's untimely demise didn't entirely deprive Western civilization of his tremendous intellectual gifts.

Against the background of Thomas Aquinas' new esthetic, John said that all of our ideas come from observing things. Today this idea seems self-evident, but it's not. Due to the tremendous influence of the ancient Greek philosopher Plato, most medieval philosophers and theologians believed that ideas preexisted in the mind and that objects merely made human beings consciously aware of them. So, for example, a man knows what an apple is only because the idea of an apple already exists in his mind. Both Augustine and Thomas Aquinas believed in variations of this idea. Augustine believed God illuminated the human mind with ideas and for this reason his theory was called illuminationism. Thomas Aquinas believed that the concept of existence, as well as other ideas, already existed in the human intellect because the mind somehow participated in God's divine intellect.

John, however, did away with this idea. In contrast to Augustine and Thomas Aquinas, he foreclosed any chance of God directly putting ideas in our heads. In philosophical language, he isolated the human intellect from receiving ideas directly from God. So where did our ideas come from? John reasoned that the ideas in our minds actually come from the objects we observe. In other words, each idea flows from the object into the human mind through the senses. This theory of knowledge seems elementary today. After all, who would deny that we learn by sight, sound, touch, taste, and smell? But in John's time, it was a game-changer.

How and why he did it is a bit technical. John came up with his idea for reasons having to do with free will. Like most of his fellow friars, John believed that mankind couldn't be greater than God because the creation couldn't be greater than the Creator. So with that in mind, he sought to show that God had free will by showing that man had free will. The difference, however, was that God had the power to do whatever he liked, even if it was absurd or defied logic, while man was limited to a finite range of choices on earth.

John, therefore, opposed Thomas Aquinas' theory regarding how human beings acquire knowledge. Thomas said that before we can choose to look at something, we must first know that there is indeed something to look at. We must first know that the thing exists. In contrast, John believed the opposite was true. He said that before we can know whether or not an object exists, we must first choose to look at it. That is to say, the first step in acquiring knowledge is an act of free will or a choice.

From this proposition, John reasoned that the idea of existence couldn't already exist in the mind as Thomas said. Rather the concept of existence must be supplied to the mind by the object being observed. And if one idea is supplied by the object, then so are all the others. All of which is to say that our ideas come from observing things. Of course John, like Thomas Aquinas, was still looking at nature to see what it could tell him about God. But that too was about to change.

The true importance of John's idea wouldn't become apparent until someone went a step further and isolated not just the intellect from God, but even the objects. And that someone was a Franciscan friar named William of Ockham. Building on John's ideas, William would finish what Thomas Aquinas had started.

William of Ockham was born around the year 1287 in the hamlet of Ockham, England, which is situated in Surrey about twenty-five miles southwest of London. As a boy, William's family gave him to the Franciscans in order for him to receive an education from the friars. He lived at the Franciscan house in London for most of his youth, attending school and training to be a friar, until he matriculated at Oxford around the year 1310. Fortunately for William, he kept his theological and philosophical views largely to himself while at Oxford. But that would last only for so long. In 1321, William left Oxford to take a job teaching philosophy at the Franciscan school in London, the *Studium generale*, where he would let everyone know just what he thought. While teaching philosophy at the *Studium generale* between 1321 and 1324, William would compose his most important works on philosophy and theology and lecture openly on his views. And that would be a problem.

William had a problem with the theologies of both Thomas Aquinas and John Duns Scotus. He believed that in both men's theologies, God was too close to man. In his view, if God was in the universe either as existence or infinite being, then God was readily at hand. Why, then, did anyone need Jesus Christ as the mediator of God's grace? If there was no meaningful separation between man and God, why did anyone need to come to God through Christ? But to oppose Aquinas and Duns Scotus was no small matter. Over the years, their ideas had won a consensus among theologians. William could be charged with heresy for opposing views that everyone seemed to accept. And a convicted heretic could be subjected to any number of punishments, including death. William, however, was undeterred.

Working largely from the theology of John Duns Scotus, William set out to put some space between man and God. His solution was quite simple. He merely applied an age-old maxim from Augustine—that God transcends space and time—to what John Duns Scotus had done. In other words, William excluded God from the Aquinas/Duns Scotus model of the cosmos. He simply moved God beyond the realm of human experience. Consequently, whereas every object once existed in God's existence or infinite being, now everything existed in empty, infinite space. The infinite canvas against which Western man apprehended everything in the universe went from being God to just space. What had once been God's existence or God's infinite being had been rendered as mere infinite space. The mental environment of the Western mind, the very background against which all things were contemplated, had been substantially changed. The connection between God, man, and nature had been severed. In William's cosmos, nature couldn't tell human beings anything about God. The knowledge that came from observing individual objects now pertained only to the objects themselves, not God. In William's philosophy, if an idea came from examining an apple, then it merely explained the apple. He had effectively made it possible to isolate every material object against the background of infinite space.

So where did God go? God remained in a heaven that transcended space and time, but which was simply off-limits to human reason because we couldn't see it or know it or otherwise experience it. According to William, man's only source for knowledge of God was the revealed truth of Holy Scripture.

William's colleagues were suspicious of his views to say the least. His philosophy was a repudiation of the entire scholastic program, which held that men could know God by reason. It was a repudiation of many of the most revered thinkers in Christendom, including Thomas Aquinas. In 1323, William was called to Bristol to explain himself before a chapter meeting of the Franciscan Order. Worse yet, someone reported him to the pope and he was summoned before the Papal Court in Avignon, France to explain his views.

When William left England for France in 1324, he couldn't have known that he would never see his home again. But it wasn't his philosophy or theology that would seal his fate. He was about to be taken down by a row between certain Franciscans and the pope. In 1328, while the investigation into his ideas was ongoing, the minister general of the Franciscan Order asked William to weigh in on the issue of apostolic poverty. It seems a contingent of Franciscans was embroiled in a fight with the pope over the question of whether Christ and the apostles owned property. The question went to the heart of the Franciscan way of life, which held that since Christ and the apostles owned absolutely nothing, those who sought to imitate Christ should likewise own nothing. In the pope's view, these anti-property Franciscans wanted to reduce the Church to a bunch of poor beggars. The pope argued that, at the very least, Christ and the apostles collectively owned the things they used. At the request of Michael Cesena, the minister general of the Franciscan Order, William examined the issue for himself, eventually becoming convinced that Christ did not own property and that the pope was a heretic for saying that he did. William had thrown his lot in with the opposition.

On May 26, 1328, William, Michael Cesena, and a handful of Franciscans fled Avignon in the still of the night to avoid charges of heresy. They made their way to Pisa, Italy where they requested asylum from Holy Roman Emperor Louis of Bavaria. Louis had already been excommunicated by the pope for assuming the throne without the pope's blessing. Meanwhile, Pope John XXII excommunicated the lot of them and ordered their arrests. In the end, Pope John never caught up with William of Ockham, Michael Cesena, or the other Franciscans. William spent the rest of his life under the emperor's protection in Munich. He died in Munich in 1347 at the age of sixty.

Yet while William died excommunicate, his ideas were never officially condemned as heresy. Moreover, in 1359, Pope Innocent VI posthumously lifted William's excommunication. So in the absence of any condemnation against William or his ideas, scholars were free to study his philosophy. And in the decades following his death, William's philosophy became increasingly popular due to its simplicity. Scholars who followed William's philosophy didn't have to look beyond the Bible for knowledge of God. Furthermore, they could approach nature in a much simpler way because the data culled from observing an individual object now pertained only to the object instead of God.

Scholasticism, however, didn't just go away. It remained the dominant school of thought in Europe's universities well into the sixteenth century. But now the genie was out of the bottle. As more and more philosophers and theologians began to assume that the fabric of the cosmos was empty space, and as they began to conceptualize each thing against this background, the twin ideas that knowledge is acquired by observing things and that those things tell us nothing about God or heaven started to appear as if they were self-evident. And as these ideas were accepted more and more as axioms, the focus of intellectual inquiry in the West began to shift from heaven to earth.

As for William, he took his philosophy a bit too far and developed an idea that isn't very popular today. He came to believe that the human senses could detect only individual objects, and that all further knowledge was merely an invention of the human mind. That is to say, he believed that human beings could have no knowledge of objective reality, but only of individual things. So, for example, dogs don't really exist. Dog is just a word people use to group certain kinds of individual animals which they think are similar. This philosophy, which became popular among British and German thinkers in the seventeenth and eighteenth centuries, came to be called nominalism.

Nonetheless, William, along with Thomas Aquinas and John Duns Scotus, had transformed the Western mind. Where the mind's eye once saw the world ordered according to hierarchies, now it was possible to conceptualize each thing separately against the background of infinite space. The effect of this new worldview was first seen in the idea that the Bible is man's only source for knowledge of God. The idea came from William of Ockham himself. Since God wasn't present in William's cosmos in a way that could be known by man, he concluded that man could know God only through the Bible. The idea was embraced and championed by Church reformers who saw in it a way to counter the authority of the Church's magisterium. Men like the fourteenth-century English reformer John Wycliffe would champion the Bible as an authority greater than the Church itself, while overlooking the fact that the Church first compiled the library of books called the Bible. And eventually, William of Ockham's idea that the Bible is the only way man can know God would become a tenet of Martin Luther's Protestant movement in the sixteenth century.

There was also a renewed interest in all things Greek and Roman. European philosophers and artists started to develop an intense interest in what the ancient Greeks and Romans had said about the material world. Philosophers began reading ancient authors with new fervor. Artists adopted scenes from Greek and Roman mythology as the subjects of their sculptures and paintings. They looked to antiquity because the ancient Greeks and Romans appeared to share their newfound interest in the natural world. But there were vast differences. With the exception of the Platonists, the pagan Greeks and Romans focused on the physical world because it was the only world they knew. They were materialists who believed in only one universe, not two. The Europeans, on the other hand, began focusing on the natural world because, according to the new worldview, the spiritual universe was now off-limits as an object of investigation. And then there was their ability to isolate objects. European philosophers and artists had the ability to isolate objects against the background of infinite space while the ancient Greeks and Romans did not. The attendant explosion of new ideas and art, however, was ascribed to a rebirth of Greco-Roman culture instead of being seen as the unique product of Christian Europe. And for this reason, this phenomenon came to be known as the Renaissance, which is from the French for rebirth.

Yet a new reverence for the Bible and a renewed interest in the ancient Greeks and Romans were relatively subdued developments compared with what was happening in art. Less than a century after the death of William of Ockham, the Italian sculptor and architect Filippo Brunelleschi discovered the rules of one-point linear perspective. He did it through a kind of cultural exchange. He took the principles contained in the *Book of Optics*, written by the eleventh-century Islamic polymath Alhazen, and applied them to the infinite space rendered by Aquinas, Duns Scotus, and Ockham. The result was astonishing! It enabled Renaissance artists like Leonardo da Vinci to do what no artist had done before—make realistic, three-dimensional representations of people and things. Seen from another viewpoint, it allowed them to construct vast three-dimensional spaces around objects. The ancient Romans never quite achieved true linear perspective in their paintings because they couldn't conceptualize the space necessary for it. In their minds, the world was made from the four elements of earth, air, water, and fire. These material elements were omnipresent in the world instead of empty space. So in their paintings, the air surrounding people and things had real substance. It was like another object occupying space, which precluded ancient painters from building accurately proportioned, three-dimensional spaces around their subjects.

The most amazing feature of Leonardo da Vinci's *The Last Supper* isn't Christ and the apostles in the foreground, but the vast space shooting into the distance behind them. Now even the simplest peasant could see the universe like Aquinas or Dante or William of Ockham. And perhaps most importantly, all of that Renaissance art in the churches, cathedrals, and public spaces did for this new worldview what the rose window did for John Scotus Eriugena's model of the cosmos and what Dante's *Divine Comedy* did for Thomas Aquinas. It disseminated the new worldview among the public.

There were, of course, early attempts at realism by artists like Giotto and Duccio. They were contemporaries of Dante who were influenced by the worldview rendered by Thomas Aquinas. Indeed, their paintings are more accurately understood as expressions of Thomist theology rather than as genuine attempts at realism. In other words, the depth in their paintings represents God's existence, not mere empty space. Working in the late thirteenth and early fourteenth centuries, they lacked the full-on ability to isolate objects that emerged with Ockham and the mathematical rules of linear perspective later developed by Brunelleschi to achieve realism like Leonardo da Vinci. Consequently, their proportions were wrong.

But while the art was esthetically stunning, there was a revolutionary shift in philosophy happening in its wake. European thinkers began studying nature in order to learn about the physical world instead of as a means of doing theology. Men like Leonardo da Vinci began observing objects to learn about nature, not God. We tend to think of Leonardo as an artist first, but he was an equally gifted natural philosopher. He was among the first to investigate how the human body actually worked by making detailed, realistic drawings of the internal human anatomy modeled after what he observed in cadavers. His art and his science went hand in hand. This was no mere coincidence. Theology and art were largely responsible for promoting the new worldview among philosophers. So first came the new worldview through theology and art; and then came a shift in the focus of intellectual inquiry from doing natural theology (studying objects to learn abut God) to doing natural philosophy (studying objects to learn about nature).

As the focus of inquiry shifted, however, natural philosophers soon realized that they needed a new guarantee of truth for their explanations of natural phenomena. Nominalists like William of Ockham had raised troubling questions regarding human understanding. It was clear that logic and reason alone couldn't guarantee that an explanation or hypothesis was true. How could a natural philosopher know that his explanation was true and not just a product of his imagination? How could he know that a nominalist like William of Ockham wasn't right? How do we know today that an explanation is objectively true and not just in agreement with our method of reasoning? The answer, of course, is that we test our explanations against observation and experimentation. And that's exactly what the natural philosophers would do as well. By testing a hypothesis over and over again to see if it produced the same result every time, the natural philosophers discovered that they could determine if their explanations were objectively true or not. Now they wouldn't be stymied by William of Ockham's assertion that knowledge of objective truth was impossible for mankind to achieve, that the natural order was merely a figment of the human imagination. Whereas men had formerly believed that logic and reason alone could guarantee truth, the practitioners of this new method of inquiry would observe, measure, and test natural phenomena in order to determine whether their explanations were actually true or not.

In the sixteenth and seventeenth centuries, brilliant men like Nicolaus Copernicus, Tycho Brahe, and Johannes Kepler applied these ideas and methods to astronomy to overturn Aristotle's idea that the earth was at the center of the universe, an idea that had been accepted as indisputable fact for more than 1,500 years. Kepler, in fact, greatly advanced our understanding of planetary motion and set the stage for the development of Newtonian physics. The great Italian astronomer Galileo Galilei went even further. Largely considered the first modern scientist, Galileo invented a kind of early scientific method of inquiry called the resoluto-compositive method. The idea was to figure out how a thing worked by breaking it down into its divisible parts. Then Galileo would examine those parts, attempt to put them back together, and record his data. He used the principles of natural philosophy to show, among other things, that not only did the earth revolve around the sun, but that it was spinning as well. Finally, there was the English statesman and philosopher Francis Bacon, who is widely esteemed as a father of the scientific method. He urged his fellow man to throw off the philosophies of the past and turn to observation and experimental testing as the source of all knowledge. He further advocated using the process of induction to develop scientific theories and laws from the particular datum culled from observation and experimental testing.

A lot had happened since Thomas Aquinas set out to solve the Aristotle problem. The esthetic transformation of the

Western mind that occurred in the thirteenth and fourteenth centuries had changed the way European philosophers, theologians, poets, playwrights, architects, and artists conceptualized heaven and earth and everything in between. Thomas Aquinas had placed everything in the universe against the background of St. Augustine's infinite space. And with that, he gave Western philosophers and theologians a way to isolate objects, particularly from the idea of hierarchies that had dominated Western thought for so long. From there, John Duns Scotus and William of Ockham carried the torch forward to isolate the intellect and objects from God, giving rise to the ideas that all of our knowledge comes from observing things and that objects only tell us about nature and not God. Ultimately, as the focus of intellectual inquiry shifted from heaven to earth, natural philosophers required a new mark of objective truth, which came with the addition of experimental testing. Here, then, were the beginnings of a method of inquiry that relied on observation and testing to study the natural world. And in time, this practice of observation plus experimental testing would become the modern scientific method of inquiry that has so profoundly transformed our world.

By the sixteenth century, Irish Christianity and its three greatest exponents—Thomas Aquinas, John Duns Scotus, and William of Ockham—had influenced religion, art, and philosophy in ways no one could have foreseen. Yet there remained one very important institution of Western civilization that had yet to be transformed—government. Emperors and kings still claimed a divine right to rule over men. They claimed that their governments were instituted by God instead of men. Now the same forces that had provided the foundation for natural philosophy and had turned the focus of inquiry from heaven to earth were about to change that too. Fittingly, the issue upon which Western Europe would turn from monarchy to democracy had been planted in Europe by the Irish monks centuries earlier. It was penance.

CHAPTER SIX

The Hidden Legacy of Irish Christianity

s the light of the Renaissance illuminated European civilization, a new darkness swept across the land. It was the Black Death. The Black Death was a form of bubonic plague that first appeared in Europe in 1347. Death rates in medieval Europe had always been high due to famine and disease, but this was different. Now millions of people were being cut down, seemingly at random, generation after generation. Men, women, children, kings and commoners alike—the plague spared no one. Between 1347 and 1350 alone, the plague killed half the population of Europe. Outbreaks of the plague devastated Europe's population until the nineteenth century. And as the bodies piled up, Christians turned to their faith for answers.

Some said the plague was a punishment from God. Still others said it was a curse from the Devil. Either way, the plague turned Christianity into a doctrine of punishments and rewards. The message was clear: Christians who followed the rules might win the favor of God and avoid the Black Death and the pains of hell, while those who didn't would surely perish in this life and the next. It was a very narrow interpretation of Christianity that offered hope in the face of hopelessness.

Those who were dying of the plague could hope for eternal life in heaven. Those who had lost family and friends to the plague could hope to see their loved ones again in paradise. And everyone else who lived in constant fear of becoming the plague's next victim could carry on in the hope that they might be spared God's wrath if they led good lives. In the mind of a sensitive boy named Martin Luther, the seed of a spiritual crisis had been sown. In time, a young boy's obsession with following the rules would become a young man's obsession with achieving spiritual perfection. And one man's spiritual crisis would become a political crisis for all of Europe.

Martin Luther was born on November 10, 1483, in Eisleben, a town in Saxony-Anhalt, Germany. The following year, his family moved to the town of Mansfeld, about five miles from Eisleben, where Luther lived until he left home for university in 1501. In the years between 1483 and 1501, two forces dominated his life and the lives of everyone around him—the Black Death and the Christian faith. Martin Luther's parents were pious and obedient Catholics; and young Martin was an obedient son and student. But for Martin Luther, obedience would ultimately prove to be a double-edged sword. In the end, Luther would be forced to choose between obedience to his father and obedience to his God.

The problem was that old Hans Luther wanted his son Martin to be a lawyer. For Hans Luther, his son's career wasn't just a matter of paternal pride. Hans and his wife Margaretta depended on their son Martin to take care of them in their old age. Hans and Margaretta were of peasant stock, the hearty descendants of those who worked the land. Yet having no land of his own, Hans Luther had been forced to earn his living in the copper mines. Eventually, Hans worked his way out of the mines to own several foundries. Meanwhile, his wife Margaretta ran the house and took care of their only son Martin.

But while Hans may have done quite well for himself, he was by no means rich. He worked hard to provide for his family and to send his son Martin to school; and he hoped his son Martin would one day return the favor. To that end, Martin Luther entered the University of Erfurt in May of 1501, at the age of seventeen. He earned his bachelor of arts degree the following year; and in 1505, he earned his master of arts degree. At the age of twenty-one, Martin Luther had completed his university education and was about to start law school; and Hans was very proud of his son indeed. But Martin would never become a lawyer. Soon young Martin Luther would discover that a man cannot serve two masters.

For a very long time, Martin Luther felt pulled between his father and his God. While his father wanted him to pursue a worldly career as a lawyer and make a respectable marriage, Martin felt an inexorable draw to serve God as a monk. This life was temporary and fleeting, he thought, but the afterlife was forever. The carnage of the Black Death undoubtedly shaped his view. Yet he couldn't bring himself to disobey his father and become a monk because the wrath of Hans had always seemed nearer than the wrath of God. Then, one sultry day in July of 1505, everything changed. Martin Luther came face to face with his mortality. On July 2, 1505, he was returning on horseback to the University of Erfurt after a brief visit with his parents in Mansfeld. Suddenly, a thunderstorm appeared in the sky. From out of nowhere, a bolt of lightening struck the earth around him and knocked him to the ground. Believing that he would surely die, he cried out,

"St. Anne help me! I will become a monk." St. Anne was his father's patron saint, the patron saint of miners.

Two weeks later Luther left the university and entered a monastery in Erfurt. The order he chose was that of St. Augustine, the reformed congregation of the Augustinians. His choice could not have been more ironic. In little more than a decade, Luther would become the first person to challenge one of Augustine's key doctrines in more than a thousand years. The only problem was that Augustine's idea had provided the basis for the authority of the Church and the state in Europe for all of that time. The two competing doctrines were a recipe for disaster, the ingredients for a spiritual and political crisis the likes of which had not been seen in the West since the fall of the Roman Empire.

Martin Luther entered the Augustinian monastery in Erfurt and set out to be an impeccable monk. He prayed and fasted and labored in earnest. He later wrote, "I was a good monk, and I kept the rule of my order so strictly that I may say that if ever a monk got to heaven by his monkery it was I." His devotion to the cowl did not go unnoticed. Brother Martin was soon chosen for the priesthood and he celebrated his first mass in 1507. It was an honor and a privilege. Not every monk was ordained a priest. His father Hans, who had been furious with his son's decision to abandon a career in the law and become a monk, attended the mass. It was a joyous occasion and Hans seemed pleased. At the very least, he seemed finally resigned to his son's decision to abandon the world for the religious life. But after the mass, Martin Luther asked his father why he had been so opposed to him becoming a monk. Hans exploded. "You learned scholar, have you never read in the Bible that you should honor your father and your mother? And here you have left me and your dear mother to look after ourselves in our old age." Martin told his father how he had been called to the monastery by a thunderbolt from the sky, to which Hans retorted, "God grant it was not an apparition of the Devil." His father's anger, however, would seem minor compared to the spiritual crisis that lay ahead.

At the heart of Martin Luther's spiritual anguish lay a kind of perfectionism. The Irish monks had originally conceived penance as a way of drawing nearer to God. But the Black Death had transformed penance from a spiritual exercise into a system of punishments and rewards. Luther and his confreres were treating it like a game. They were doing penance to win heaven and avoid hell. Yet of all the monks in the monastery, Martin Luther's view of penance was perhaps the most peculiar. Luther believed that in order to avoid hell, all of his sins had to be forgiven; and in order for all of his sins to be forgiven, every sin had to be confessed. But whereas other monks assumed that God's forgiveness included even those sins that couldn't be remembered, Luther believed that if he forgot to confess even one sin, his soul would be condemned to hell. In short, a kind of perfectionism crept into Luther's spirituality. It's really not surprising that perfectionism lay at the heart of his spiritual torment. For it was also perfectionism that caused Augustine to abandon Manichaeism and embrace the idea of original sin more than a thousand years earlier. And the Irish monks had originally developed the penitentials to counter the perfectionism that crept into Augustine's theology as a result of having only public penance. As for Martin Luther, he spent hours at confession trying to remember even the smallest offense. The tedium of it all eventually got to his confessor when he told Luther, "Look here, if you expect Christ to forgive you, come in with something to forgive—parricide, blasphemy, adultery—instead of all these peccadilloes."

Luther fixated on his peculiar problem for years, mostly because like Augustine he had to overcome his own pride before he abandoned his quest for perfection. He had hoped that a trip to Rome in November of 1510 might help, but it didn't. Even in Rome, Christians had come to see penance in terms of punishments and rewards. Luther returned to Erfurt in April of 1511 unhappier than ever. If he couldn't find the answer he was seeking in Rome, then where? He felt hopeless. Fortunately, that same month, Luther was transferred to the town of Wittenberg to teach at its university. The new university at Wittenberg was the pride and joy of Prince Frederick the Wise, ruler of Saxony. University life was a welcome break for Luther if only because it took his mind off of his seeming lack of spiritual progress. He earned his doctor of theology there in 1512; and he lectured on Holy Scripture from 1513 to 1517. It was the first time Martin Luther scrupulously studied the Bible. And there too at Wittenberg, he met Johann von Staupitz, the vicar of the Augustinian Order. Staupitz would become a kind of mentor to Luther, introducing him to the philosophy of William of Ockham and certain ideas of Christian mysticism. In time, Luther would use these ideas to interpret what he read in Scripture and to develop a solution to his penance problem that would shake Western Europe to its core.

By 1517, Martin Luther had been quietly teaching and developing his ideas at Wittenberg for four years. Meanwhile in Rome, a massive construction project was underway that would ultimately cost the Catholic Church Northern Europe. The Protestant Reformation actually started over a flap between Martin Luther and the pope about how the Church was raising money to build St. Peter's Basilica in Rome. Today, St. Peter's is the largest church in the world. Thousands of people visit it each year as pilgrims or tourists to behold its majesty and to take in its priceless works of art by Renaissance masters like Michelangelo and Bernini. But back in 1517, construction of the great church had just begun. Construction started in 1506 under Pope Julius II and wasn't completed until 1626. Julius died in 1513 and left Pope Leo X to carry on the work. And what Leo needed more than anything to keep his pet project rolling along was money. So he turned to a source of revenue that the Church had long used to fund construction projects—indulgences.

The trade in indulgences during the Late Middle Ages and the Renaissance is infamous. According to Catholic doctrine, an indulgence shortens a person's time spent in purgatory. An indulgence does not forgive sin, nor does it excuse future sin, nor is an indulgence granted in exchange for money. Indulgences are granted for enumerated acts of faith. For example, a Catholic today is granted a partial or plenary indulgence for reading the Bible. But in 1517, indulgences were being granted in exchange for donations to all kinds of Church causes, including the construction of St. Peter's Basilica in Rome. To make matters worse, the Church claimed the indulgence for St. Peter's conferred fantastic spiritual benefits such as forgiving all of the purchaser's sins, granting him entry into heaven, and freeing his dead relatives from purgatory. Simply put, indulgences were being abused.

The lead salesman for the indulgence for St. Peter's was a Dominican friar named Johann Tetzel. He was a marketing genius, coining the slogan, "As soon as the coin in the coffer rings the soul from purgatory springs." Tetzel, along with an army of fellow vendors, went from town to town with their letters of indulgence from the pope, granting them to anyone who gave to the cause. It was quite a racket. And it was forbidden in Wittenberg where Luther lived because it competed with the indulgences that Prince Frederick sold. Still, many of Luther's parishioners traveled to neighboring towns to receive the indulgence for St. Peter's. When word finally got back to Luther as to the fantastic benefits the indulgence promised, he decided enough was enough. He resolved to stop the abuse before it went too far.

On October 31, in the year 1517, Martin Luther took quill in hand and furiously set down ninety-five propositions, or theses, on paper against the abusive trade in indulgences. Then he marched down to the Castle Church, nailed his complaint to its large, wooden door, and returned home. He wasn't looking for a fight. He was looking for a debate among his fellow theologians. The church door served as a kind of bulletin board for the university. Faculty and students commonly nailed theological questions for debate to the church door. Moreover, Luther had written his complaint in Latin, a language that only learned men were able to read. His words were almost certainly not intended for the public's eyes. Little did he know that his personal grievances with the Church would soon be translated into German for all the world to see. Little did he know that his few sheets of paper would cast Christian Europe into utter chaos.

The thrust of Luther's complaint was that the pope didn't have the authority to sell forgiveness or release souls from purgatory. And just to make sure his complaint wasn't ignored by the powers that be, he also sent a copy of his complaint to his archbishop, Albert of Mainz, who was the Church official directly responsible for the abusive indulgence trade in the German lands. In turn, the archbishop sent a copy to the pope. But what Luther didn't expect was that his ninety-five theses would be translated into German and distributed to the public. Soon Luther's complaint had gone well beyond a mere theological debate. Common people, not just the clergy and other learned men, started to take sides.

The pope summoned Luther to Rome to answer charges of heresy, but Luther had the support and promise of Prince Frederick the Wise that he would not be taken to Rome. So began three years of negotiations by Prince Frederick to have Luther tried by a council of German princes headed by the Holy Roman Emperor. In the meantime, Luther was compelled to explain himself to officials from the Church, heads of state, scholars, theologians, and the public. Indeed, he engaged in public debate and wrote extensively on his theological views before his trial in 1521. And here was where the Church badly erred.

By pursuing Luther as a heretic, the Church opened a Pandora's box. In the beginning, Luther was concerned only with reforming indulgences. But once he was charged with heresy, Luther was forced to defend himself. So he participated in a public debate and wrote extensively on his views in order to garner support. And in the course of doing that, he set loose the doctrines that would prove so damaging to the authority of the Church. What's more, his alleged heresy, his theological writings, his opponents' vitriol, his sermons and public debate, and his trial all made him into a celebrity. In the eyes of the people, he was David and the Catholic Church was Goliath.

Rome even made the situation worse by attempting to intimidate him. Every time the pope accused Luther of heresy for disobeying the Church, Luther responded by calling the pope a heretic for disobeying Scripture. Rome's intransigence merely fueled the Protestant fire. One wonders what might have been had the Church simply given in to Luther's original demand to reform indulgences.

But Prince Frederick couldn't protect Luther forever. Ultimately, Martin Luther was forced to stand trial for heresy. He appealed to Holy Roman Emperor Charles V for a hearing before a secular council. And after much political wrangling, Prince Frederick and other supporters of Luther succeeded in having the case transferred from Rome to Germany. This meant Luther would be tried before a council of German princes instead of by the cardinals in Rome.

Luther requested a hearing from the emperor because he believed the Church was too biased to fairly judge the case. Moreover, he believed the emperor had a duty to save the Church from worldly corruption by depriving it of worldly power. The emperor, however, took jurisdiction over the case for reasons that were more political than spiritual. The princes elected the emperor and for this reason they were called electors. As the German lands became increasingly divided against the Church, the emperor and the electors needed to show the people that they were still in control. Plus the crisis presented a good opportunity for the electors to steal some political power back from the Church, like stopping Rome from taking money out of their lands in the form of tithes and donations.

On April 17, 1521, Martin Luther appeared before an imperial council or diet, at the German city of Worms, to answer charges of heresy. Prince Frederick had obtained a guarantee of safe passage for Luther, by which the emperor promised he would not be harmed while traveling to and from the hearing. Luther's appearance before the Diet of Worms, as it came to be called, lasted two days. By then the pope had excommunicated Luther, but the council didn't know that. One of the prosecutors, a man named Jerome Aleander, withheld the document condemning Luther because it also condemned a man named Ulrich von Hutten. Hutten was a knight and a German nationalist who wanted to implement Luther's reforms by launching a military crusade in the German lands; and the prosecutor was afraid Hutten might start an insurrection upon learning that he too had been excommunicated. If the diet had known that Rome had already condemned Luther of heresy, it would have deferred to the pope. But it didn't know that and so Luther was forced to defend himself against heresy by explaining his views to the princes. At his trial before the German nobility, one of the prosecutors finally asked him, "I ask you, Martin—answer candidly and without horns—do you or do you not repudiate your books and the errors which they contain?"

"Since then Your Majesty and your lordships desire a simple reply," he responded, "I will answer without horns and without teeth. Unless I am convicted by Scripture and plain reason—I do not accept the authority of popes and councils, for they have contradicted each other—my conscience is captive to the Word of God. I cannot and I will not recant anything, for to go against conscience is neither right nor safe. Here I stand, I cannot do otherwise."

The emperor wanted to condemn Luther for heresy the next day, but he needed the backing of the princes. That took about a month to get, which was why the Edict of Worms condemning Luther and ordering his arrest didn't issue until

May 26. Yet only four of the six electors signed the Edict of Worms. Prince Frederick the Wise was one of the two noblemen who didn't sign. In fact, he conspired to save Luther from punishment by hiding him in a castle. He had Luther abducted on the road back to Wittenberg and spirited to Wartburg Castle in Thuringia. Luther spent almost a year in hiding at the castle, spending his time writing about theology and translating the Bible into German. Meanwhile, Europe was on fire. People were walking away from the Church in droves. Clergy were abandoning their vocations, monasteries and convents were growing empty, mobs were vandalizing churches, and peasants were rising in revolt against the nobility. The very fabric of European civilization was coming undone. So what exactly had Martin Luther said that caused so much trouble?

In the course of fighting the powers that be over indulgences, Luther dragged out his one big idea for everyone to see. Using the new worldview, he treated the human body in the same way that William of Ockham treated any material object. He isolated the body from the soul and reasoned that the body couldn't possibly have anything to do with sin or salvation. In Luther's view, the soul was the part of man that sinned and was forgiven. The soul was the part of man that went to heaven or hell. The body, on the other hand, had nothing to do with it. The body was merely the costume of mortality that human beings wore during their lives on earth. In his 1520 treatise entitled *The Freedom of a Christian*, Luther wrote,

> *It is evident that no external thing has any influence*
> *in producing Christian righteousness or freedom, or*
> *in producing unrighteousness or servitude....What*

> *can it profit the soul if the body is well, free, and*
> *active, and eats, drinks, and does as it pleases?...*
> *On the other hand, how will poor health or impris-*
> *onment or hunger or thirst or any other external*
> *misfortune harm the soul?*

For Luther, the body was merely a vehicle for the soul just as an automobile is merely a vehicle for its driver. To extend the analogy, the driver steers the car. The car doesn't steer the driver. Luther wrote, "Good works do not make a good man, but a good man does good works; evil works do not make a wicked man, but a wicked man does evil works."

By isolating the body from the soul, Luther had solved his spiritual crisis. His idea that the body had nothing to do with the soul explained why he had failed to achieve spiritual perfection with penance. In Luther's new interpretation of the sacrament, no amount of penance could have any effect on the soul whatsoever. Thus penance was futile. All of which led to his famous dictum of the Protestant Reformation that justification, or righteousness in the sight of God, is by faith alone in Christ. And by faith, Luther meant mere belief. Luther no longer needed to be perfect because, he reasoned, Christ was perfect for him. All he needed to do was believe. But in as much as Luther solved one problem, he created quite another. With his big idea, Luther undermined the theological foundation of the doctrine of the Two Powers. And in so doing, he undermined the very authority of the Church and the state in Europe.

Luther's big idea was a cultural bombshell. Luther was the first person to challenge Augustine's doctrines supporting the definition of the Church as the living Body of Christ on earth.

In effect, Luther was saying that the Church was not identical with Christ. And in saying that, he undermined the principle that in order to be in communion with Christ, a person had to be in communion with the Church. This tenet of the faith had been the bedrock of the Church's spiritual and political authority in Europe for more than a thousand years. It was the bedrock of the doctrine of the Two Powers, the political theory articulated by Pope Gelasius I in 494 that enunciated not only the power of the Church and its clergy, but the power of emperors and kings as well. In so many words, the doctrine of the Two Powers said that God gave the Church the power to save men's souls, and he gave the emperor the privilege of using force in order to protect men from themselves; and of these two powers, the spiritual power was the greater. Luther's doctrine of justification by faith alone, however, challenged the tenet that the Church and its clergy mediated God's grace *in persona Christi* or in the person of Christ. And it all hinged on a new idea that was foreign to Augustine and Aquinas—the idea that the body had nothing to do with the soul. But what Luther never understood was that if the pope had no power from God to rule over men's souls, then neither did kings have any power from God to rule over their bodies.

After almost a year spent in hiding at Wartburg Castle, Luther returned to Wittenberg only to find he had unleashed utter chaos. In his own hometown, monks had abandoned the monastery, nuns had fled the convent, and citizens had vandalized the local church believing it stood for evil and corruption. But the worst was yet to come. In light of Luther's theology, some people concluded that the hierarchies of the Church and the state were creations of man, not God; and therefore the social inequality that was the product of those hierarchies was manifestly unjust. This was the spark that ignited the Peasant's War of 1524-1525.

Discontent among the German peasantry had been simmering for at least a century before Luther. Then along came a man named Thomas Müntzer, a contemporary of Luther who preached a radicalized version of Luther's theology. In Müntzer's view, the notion that the hierarchies of the Church and the state were merely inventions of man was reason enough to abolish the old social order. But Müntzer's cure was worse than the disease. Müntzer didn't believe all men were created equally free. Referring back to Augustine's doctrine of the total depravity of man, he believed all men were created equally enslaved to sin. Thus he wanted to replace the Church and the state with a theocracy ruled by a special Christian elect. So instead of having a king who was ordained by God to rule over men, Müntzer intended to transfer that power to a group of Christians who could lay claim to having attained salvation.

Fueled by Müntzer's call for a more equal society, the peasants formed a frenzied mob to demand an end to their serfdom. When Emperor Charles V completely ignored their demands in 1524, some 300,000 peasants throughout Germany, as well as in parts of Austria and Switzerland, took up arms against the government. Müntzer himself led the revolt in Luther's own province of Saxony. It didn't go well for the peasants. By the summer of 1525, some 100,000 of them had been killed in battle or executed. The revolt had been crushed. As for Thomas Müntzer, it didn't go well for him either. He was captured on May 15, 1525, and was tortured and beheaded.

Martin Luther, on the other hand, went on to lead a full and productive life. In 1525, he married a runaway nun named Katharina von Bora who was sixteen years his junior.

Together they had six children of their own and adopted four others. He called Wittenberg home for the rest of his life. There he raised his family, taught at the university, expounded upon his beliefs, and continued to lead the movement he started. Yet none of this would have been possible had it not been for the support of the nobility. The Edict of Worms against Luther was never repealed, but neither was it ever enforced because he had the support of noblemen like Price Frederick the Wise. They not only protected him from the long arm of Rome, but their support ensured the success of the Protestant movement. In Luther's own lifetime, Norway, Sweden, Denmark, the Netherlands, Scotland, England, and much of Germany and Switzerland broke with Rome and converted to various forms of Protestantism. Luther's ideas found favor with European heads of state not only because they believed he was right about God and man, but also because his theology seemed to augment their power. Particularly, Luther provided the key idea they needed in order to refute the Church's claims of supremacy over their rule under the doctrine of the Two Powers.

Yet all that glitters is not gold. The kings of Europe would ultimately fare no better than the pope in the wake of Luther's new theology. In time, all of them, Protestant and Catholic alike, would be either abolished or reduced to tourist attractions. When Martin Luther died on February 18, 1546, the political ramifications of his theology had yet to be fully realized. However, it was only a matter of time before the divine right of kings to rule over men was finished. The Peasant's War gave the European monarchs a preview of what was to come. The power of popes and kings had long been predicated on the doctrine of the Two Powers. And by operation of the doctrine, if the pope had no power, then neither did the king. If God's grace was available to every person directly by faith alone, then what made a king special? Any believer or assembly of believers could claim to be qualified in the eyes of God to wield the power of the sword. Any believer could claim to be doing God's will in upholding the law, meting out justice, and protecting sinners from themselves. Luther never went that far, but his ideas opened the door to it. Suddenly, participation in civil life became a way of doing God's will for thousands of people who would have otherwise done God's will in monasteries and churches. From here, Western civilization's journey from monarchy to theocracy to modern democracy was a bloody one. It was the journey from John Calvin to John Locke.

While Martin Luther won legions of supporters in his stand against the Church, the Reformation he sparked was by no means a unified movement. For example, unlike Thomas Müntzer, Martin Luther didn't believe government should be run according to the Bible. Luther thought theocracy as a form of government asked the impossible of its citizens. First, he believed no man could be compelled to faith by force. Only God, by his saving grace, brought men to faith. And second, he believed the Christian life was very rarely achieved even among those with faith. A government run by the Book, therefore, would fail to serve most people because most people would fail to serve it. In essence, he was against perfectionism. So Luther was content merely to have a ruler like Prince Frederick the Wise secure the peace and maintain the public order.

Nevertheless, theocracy was becoming increasingly popular among certain Protestants as a replacement for the doctrine of the Two Powers. This was particularly true in Switzerland where provinces and towns were governed by councils instead of kings. The reason for this was simple. Church and state naturally converged in Protestant theology. Whereas Augustine had affirmed the definition of the Catholic Church as the living Body of Christ on earth, Luther and other reformers defined their churches as the community of believers. Under this definition, the same people who made up the church also made up the city council. The separation between the Church and the state throughout the Middle Ages had always depended on the distinct powers of the clergy and the king. Now the new theology eliminated that distinction.

The leader of the Reformation in Switzerland was a young priest named Ulrich Zwingli. Zwingli was born in the Swiss village of Wildhaus in 1484. He studied at the University of Vienna and the University of Basel, and was ordained a priest in 1506. He was drawn to reforming the Catholic Church by the ideas of the Catholic philosopher and theologian Erasmus of Rotterdam. Erasmus didn't want to abandon the sacraments like some reformers, but merely wanted to restore their meaning. Erasmus thought Catholicism had become too legalistic, that the emphasis was on rules and rituals instead of individual spiritual transformation. He saw a lot of people going through the motions of receiving the sacraments, but little evidence of spiritual transformation. He believed salvation was unique to human beings and that it happened in the soul rather than in the external spaces of some church or cathedral. After all, the sacraments meant nothing if they didn't transform men's souls. To a young priest named Ulrich Zwingli, Erasmus' idea of internal spiritual transformation resonated like a struck bell. Eventually, Zwingli combined the ideas of Erasmus with those of Martin Luther to create his own take on Christianity. But Zwingli differed from Erasmus and Martin Luther on a key point—free will. Erasmus and Martin Luther believed human beings had the power to reach out to Christ. If nothing else, human beings could at least choose to believe. Zwingli, however, did not think human beings could choose to believe. He piled on Augustine's doctrines of total depravity and predestination. In Zwingli's philosophy, the only way a man could come to faith in Christ was if the Holy Spirit made it happen. This was why Zwingli and the multitudes he influenced called themselves the elect, because they believed they had been earmarked for salvation by God. People who believe in predestination almost always assume they are truly the elect.

It's difficult to know exactly how information and ideas flowed among Protestant circles at the time. But one can certainly see these ideas in other reformers like Thomas Müntzer. These ideas marked a division within the Protestant movement between those like Zwingli and those like Luther. Politically, Zwingli and the elect departed from the Lutherans in believing God had ordained them to rule over both church and state. After all, why should God give that power to the pope or some king who wasn't saved? In fact, Zwingli's push for theocracy divided Switzerland along religious lines and nearly led to civil war. Zwingli eventually became a prominent citizen of Zurich and convinced the city council to adopt his brand of religion; and from there, several other Swiss states converted from Catholicism to Zwingli's brand of Protestantism. Alarmed by this phenomenon, another group of Swiss states formed an alliance in order to protect themselves from

194 | THE SECRET GOSPEL OF IRELAND

Zwingli's Reformation. Tensions mounted over the course of several years; and in 1531, the alliance attacked Zurich. Ulrich Zwingli died in the fighting on October 9, 1531, at the age of forty-seven. But his passion for Protestant theocracy would live on in John Calvin.

John Calvin certainly didn't invent the idea of Protestant theocracy, but he wrote about it in a way that would become wildly popular with Protestants throughout Europe and America. John Calvin lived at a time when people still believed that government's authority to rule over men derived from God, which was why theology necessarily had political implications. So in writing the world's first systematic treatment of Protestant theology, Calvin also expounded an alternative to the doctrine of the Two Powers. Martin Luther had already undermined the doctrine of the Two Powers. Now John Calvin would offer up a challenger.

The son of a lawyer, John Calvin was born on July 10, 1509, in France. After a lengthy education in theology and the law, he followed in his father's footsteps to become a lawyer in 1532.

The next year, in 1533, he experienced a religious conversion. He had suddenly found God and wanted to reform the Catholic Church. But the Church in France wasn't amenable to reform. The king and the bishops liked things just the way they were. So in 1534, Calvin converted to Protestantism.

By 1535, Calvin was a heretic by French standards. He had been accused of involvement in heretical activities by the French authorities and risked punishment if he stayed in France. So Calvin fled Paris for the Protestant city of Basel, Switzerland, which had been one of Zwingli's strongholds several years earlier. And there in 1536, he published his monumental treatise on Protestant theology, *Institutes of the Christian Religion*.

Basel, however, would not be John Calvin's laboratory of theocracy. That distinction would ultimately go to the city of Geneva. Calvin came to Geneva by accident in 1536. Within the space of a few months, Calvin traveled from Basel to Italy and then back to Paris. The French had offered heretics amnesty if they reconciled with the Church. But in the end, Calvin decided not to take it and fled Paris for the city of Strasbourg. En route, Calvin was forced to make a detour to avoid running into the French army. He ended up in Geneva for the night and was invited to help reform the Church there. He stayed for more than a year. Calvin's reforms included using government to enforce a strict religious code of conduct. This, however, proved so unpopular with the people that Calvin was expelled from the city in 1537. They probably should have read his book first.

John Calvin spent the next few years in Strasbourg where he met his wife Idelette de Bure. Actually, he didn't meet her so much as she was found for him. When it looked as though he might stay single for the rest of his life, Calvin's friends pressed him to find a wife. They made all of the usual arguments that might sway a man in favor of marriage—he needed a cook, he needed a housekeeper, he needed someone to wait on him from head to toe, he needed someone to give him children. Eventually, Calvin relented and his friends formed a search committee to find John a wife. For his part, Calvin told his friends that he would like to marry a woman who was just like himself, but who also enjoyed making him the center of her life while doing all of the chores he despised. Calvin might have been a remarkable theologian, but he was also just a man. On those orders, Calvin's friends spent a year and a half looking for a mate before finally abandoning their quest and settling for a real woman. In the end, Calvin married a widow who already had two children. She had been an Anabaptist with her previous husband, which was a Protestant sect that Calvin would persecute throughout his life. Nevertheless, Calvin and Idelette appeared to have a happy and loving marriage. In the ensuing years, they had three children together. Tragically, their first child died at two weeks and the other two died at birth. And then, a mere nine years after they had married, Idelette died and Calvin was alone again. But all of that was yet to happen. For the time being, Calvin earned a living as a minister, updated his *Institutes*, wrote a commentary on Paul's Letter to the Romans, and enjoyed married life. It seemed he might spend his career in Strasbourg. But then Geneva wanted him back.

By 1541, Geneva was at risk of going Catholic. The population had largely stopped attending church and Rome extended an olive branch by inviting the city to return to Catholicism. In response, the city council sought a first-rate theologian to fend off Rome's advance. And when their first choice refused the job, they asked John Calvin to come back. Calvin returned to Geneva with carte blanche for his reforms; and about two months later the city passed the Ecclesiastical Ordinances. These laws set forth the structure of the Reformed Church and established an ecclesiastical court called the Consistory, which had jurisdiction over religious offenses and disputes. Those who openly opposed the Reformed Church or its doctrines were either exiled or executed. This merger of church and state made perfect sense to Calvin. He wrote, "...that no idolatry, no blasphemy against the name of God, no calumnies against his truth, nor other offenses to religion, break out and be disseminated among the people...in short, that a public form of religion may exist among Christians, and humanity among men." So what was this "public form of religion" of which he wrote?

Like all Protestant theocracies, it was a form of perfectionism that was destined to breed misery and spark change. Calvin's theology was a synthesis of Augustine, Ockham, Luther, and Zwingli, with the Bible acting as the mediator for all knowledge of Christ and God. What he ended up with was an interpretation of Christianity where God's elect were baptized into a state of grace; which was sustained by repeatedly coming back to the Bible through public sermons; and which was enforced by the state.

Since the Calvinists believed the Bible was mankind's only source for knowledge of Christ and God, it became the de facto mediator of God's grace. Calvin wrote, "The sinner receives forgiveness by the ministry of the Church; in other words, not without the preaching of the gospel. And of what nature is this preaching? That we are washed from our sins by the blood of Christ." To this end, Calvin ordered that public sermons be held throughout Geneva several times each week. Attendance was mandatory. It truly was a way of life, a public form of religion.

John Calvin lived in Geneva until his death in 1564. During that time, Geneva became hugely influential among Protestants in Europe as a hub of Calvinist thought. Notable visitors included British reformers John Knox and William Whittingham. They carried Calvin's theology and theocracy back to Britain where it became the foundation of the Scottish Presbyterian, Congregationalist, and Puritan movements. William Whittingham even married Calvin's sister and presided over one of the most influential English translations of the Bible, fittingly known as the Geneva Bible because it was written in Geneva. But if Geneva was a laboratory of theocracy, then Britain was a laboratory of democracy. In Britain, theocracy and monarchy would collide in a violent pageant of persecutions and civil wars. Calvinism and the divine right of kings would smash together like atoms in a supercollider to produce the essential element of modern Western democracy—the social contract.

On the continent, theology sparked the Reformation. But in England, the spark that lit the fire of the Reformation wasn't theology. It was politics. In contrast to the Lutheran and Calvinist Churches, the Church of England went from Catholic to Protestant because of a change of leadership, not a change of doctrine. The king split with Rome and declared himself head of the Church. The short version goes something like this: King Henry VIII wanted a divorce; the pope refused; spurred on by Protestant reformers, the king broke with Rome in 1534 and declared himself Supreme Head of the Church of England. There were of course some theological differences, but they were relatively minor. All in all, it still looked like the Catholic Church, but with the king at its helm instead of the pope. The doctrine of the Two Powers wasn't abolished or replaced. The Two Powers were merely consolidated in one man, the king. To this day, the British monarch remains the head of the Church of England. Queen Elizabeth II, however, has considerably less power over her subjects than Henry VIII did, mostly because of what happened next.

In the wake of Henry's split with Rome, Britain was left with the Roman Catholic Church, the near-Catholic Church of England headed by the king, and a boatload of Calvinists. It was a recipe for disaster. Each group believed it had cornered the market on salvation and that everyone else was going to hell. To make matters worse, each group believed their religion should be the official state religion like Roman Catholicism had been before the Reformation. Even the various Calvinist sects didn't get along with one another. A mixture of Presbyterians, Congregationalists, and Puritans, some wanted to take the reins of government while others sought to secede entirely from society.

The Presbyterians, Congregationalists, and Puritans all shared similar Calvinist beliefs. The difference between them, however, was mainly in how their churches were organized. Presbyterian churches, for example, were organized within a hierarchy. Congregationalist churches, on the other hand, were usually loosely affiliated with other congregations or totally independent. Many Puritans, believing they were the elect, wanted to separate from all other churches so as to not contaminate their worship. Some Puritans even headed for Massachusetts in 1620 and 1630 where they attempted to establish a "City upon a Hill." The popular line is that they fled England in search of religious freedom. In fact, they went to America to establish a theocracy in accordance with their Calvinist beliefs. They would have found Thomas Jefferson's ideas on individual liberty completely abhorrent. In Puritan New England, for example, it was against the law for a man to kiss his wife on Sunday.

The years after Henry's split from Rome were filled with turmoil as Christians battled Christians for the prize of Britain. Henry's successors included Edward VI (1537-1553), a Protestant king who tried to make the Church of England look less Catholic by abolishing the rule of clerical celibacy and ordering mass said in English instead of Latin. Next came the Catholic queen Mary I (1553–1558), nicknamed Bloody Mary by her Protestant detractors for her brutal persecutions against them. Then there was Queen Elizabeth I (1558–1603), a Protestant queen who brutally persecuted Catholics. Indeed, she was bloodier than Bloody Mary. James I (1603–1625) gained a reputation for brutally persecuting Catholics and Protestants alike. He wasn't about to lose his divine right to rule to the Catholics or to the followers of John Calvin. Finally, there was the quasi-Catholic king Charles I (1625–1649).

Charles I insisted, up until the bitter end, that he had a divine and absolute right to rule over every man, woman, and child in Britain. He believed he was an agent of God. The problem for Charles, however, was that by the time he became king in 1625, the British Parliament was filled with Calvinists who begged to differ on the divine status of their king. Indeed, the Calvinists in Britain had long believed their Anglican kings and queens were just too close to being Catholic; and Charles gave good cause for their concern.

He was, in fact, a Protestant king with heavily Catholic leanings. His queen was a Catholic from France. He used Irish Catholic troops against Scottish Calvinists when they rebelled against his attempts to seize greater control over the Church of Scotland. His efforts to support Protestants against Catholics during the Thirty Years War seemed half-hearted. And when Catholics in Ireland turned against their Protestant overlords in 1641, it looked as though the king was sympathetic to the Catholic side. Added to this, the king repeatedly dissolved Parliament whenever it voiced opposition to his plans; and he used the secretive Court of Star Chamber to prosecute his enemies.

The British Parliament had long been a non-binding advisory committee to the king. But now the members of Parliament wanted more power to at least safeguard their Calvinist lifestyle. The long-standing conflict between the Calvinist Parliament and the Anglican monarch was, at its core, religious. Since 1549, the English monarch had attempted to rein in the Calvinists and their public form of religion by forcing them to use the Book of Common Prayer at their worship services. It was a script for the liturgy issued by the archbishop of Canterbury and approved by the king. The king was telling the Calvinists exactly what to preach and how to worship instead of letting them preach from the Bible according to their beliefs. And it was meant to remind the Calvinists that the king was God's representative on earth.

In 1641, members of Parliament had had enough of their divinely ordained king. They presented Charles with a list of grievances which has come to be known as the Grand Remonstrance. Charles refused to settle the grievances in the way Parliament requested and he softly reasserted his absolute power over the state as king of England. Two weeks later, on January 5, 1642, Charles made an error which would cost him his life. He ordered the arrest of five members of Parliament for treason, alleging they had colluded with Scottish forces against the Crown. And it was true. They had in fact colluded with Scottish forces against the Crown. But Charles entered the House of Commons by force to make the arrests. He was the first and last British monarch to ever do so. It was an act akin to the president of the United States entering the United States Congress by force to arrest five of its members. It represented a complete breakdown of government and stripped Charles of his legitimacy as king. To add insult to injury, Charles wasn't even able to make the arrests. The five alleged traitors had been forewarned of their arrests and were absent. Parliament responded by immediately seizing control of London. The king fled the city, marshaled his troops against Parliament, and the English Civil War had begun.

There were no freedom fighters in the English Civil War. Nobody was fighting for individual liberty. Each side was fighting to impose its rule and its religious beliefs. In the end, Charles lost the war to the forces of Parliament, which were led by a brilliant military strategist and tactician named Oliver Cromwell. Cromwell was himself a member of Parliament, a Congregationalist, and a religious fanatic. He was also a monster who would go on to murder thousands of his own countrymen and commit genocide in Ireland. He truly hated Catholics, believing the Catholic Church was the Antichrist, and he was no fan of the Church of England either. Cromwell rose to power by reforming and controlling the army; and by 1645, he had defeated the bulk of the king's forces. He created a professional, full-time fighting force instead of relying on the usual practice of assembling a patchwork of noble dilettantes and conscripts as the need arose. He was terribly effective too. In 1646, Charles surrendered to the Scots. A few years later, on January 20, 1649, the king was tried for treason. King Charles I was subsequently found guilty, sentenced to death, and beheaded ten days later on January 30, 1649. It was the beginning of the end for the divine right of kings. For how could the king have been beheaded if he was truly the agent of God? What justified putting him on trial for treason and having him executed like a common criminal? And what was the basis for the authority of government if not God? The answer was man; and the man who had the answer was Thomas Hobbes.

Thomas Hobbes was an English philosopher. He fled England for Paris in 1640, two years before the start of the English Civil War. Tensions between Parliament and the king had been steadily mounting; and Hobbes, as a prominent supporter of the king, feared that the Puritans might try to kill him. Hobbes would spend the next eleven years in Paris, watching the English Civil War from the sidelines while working on his masterpiece *Leviathan*. With *Leviathan*, Hobbes became the first person in the West to articulate a new theory of government since the doctrine of the Two Powers. In it, Hobbes rejected the idea that government is ordained by God to rule over men. Instead, he argued that government is created by men and rules by the consent of the governed. Hobbes' concept of consent, however, was colored by his view of human nature. Hobbes believed men were naturally born free. But without the power of government to restrain their absolute liberty, he believed that human beings invariably did violence against one another in order to survive. He believed men were motivated by the desire for power and the fear of death. Hence, like Plato, he believed democracy gave too much license to mankind's destructive tendencies. His state of nature was a kind of law of the jungle or survival of the fittest, a world where materialism met original sin. Of it, he wrote,

> *In such condition there is no place for industry; because the fruit thereof is uncertain: and consequently no culture of the earth; no navigation, nor use of the commodities that may be imported by sea; no commodious building; no instruments of moving, and removing, such things as require much force; no knowledge of the face of the earth; no account of*

> *time; no arts; no letters; no society; and which is worst of all, continual fear, and danger of violent death; and the life of man, solitary, poor, nasty, brutish, and short.*

And so for Hobbes, consent more closely meant submission or acquiescence than agreement. It was the voluntary submission of each man's will to one man or assembly of men in order to secure protection from force and fraud by other men. In order to achieve this end, Hobbes advocated a strong central government like absolute monarchy. He didn't believe democracy was up to the job of protecting men from each other. Nevertheless, his basic idea that government is by the consent of the governed, and not ordained by God, remains with us today. At its heart is the idea that only individual persons have rights. In turn, individuals loan their God-given rights to government in order to secure certain benefits like protection from harm. This arrangement has come to be known as the social contract, and it is the theory upon which modern Western democracy rests. For replacing the divine right of kings with the idea of the social contract, *Leviathan* represents a milestone in human thought.

Yet Hobbes didn't have to reach very far for his ideas on government. Hobbes was a natural philosopher and one of the first of the great English empiricists. In philosophy, empiricism is the belief that all knowledge is derived from sense-experience. Hobbes worked for Francis Bacon for a short time and later formed a personal relationship with Galileo, from whom he learned the resoluto-compositive method. The resoluto-compositive method was an early kind of scientific method developed by Galileo. Basically, Galileo believed he could learn how a thing worked by taking it apart and putting it back together. Accordingly, Hobbes took all he had learned as a natural philosopher and empiricist and applied it to the study of man and government.

Hobbes began his analysis by characterizing government as an organism or a body. Naturally, he excluded the idea that government was ordained by God to rule over men because he couldn't observe God. And having ruled out God, the only possible explanation for the existence of government was that it was created by man. Hobbes therefore concluded that all of the rights that seem to belong to the sovereign must really belong to the individual who consents to be governed by the sovereign. In other words, only individual persons have rights. Government, if it has any power at all, must borrow its power from those who naturally possess it. Astonishingly, it would seem the concepts of natural rights and the sovereignty of the individual are byproducts of isolating government from God.

Hobbes published *Leviathan* in 1651. That same year, Oliver Cromwell invited Hobbes back to England, mostly because Hobbes possessed the only theory of government that could justify Parliament's rule. After King Charles I was beheaded in 1649, a period of social discord ensued called the engagement controversy. England didn't have a legitimate government and both sides—Puritans and Royalists—were trying to force people to accept or renounce Parliament. Amidst the turmoil, Oliver Cromwell took control of the country and appointed a Parliament of like-minded men to make a new constitution. However, they were never able to come to an agreement as to just what that constitution should say. Finally, when Parliament tried to dissolve Cromwell's army in 1653, Cromwell dissolved Parliament instead and appointed himself Lord Protector of the Commonwealth of England, Scotland, and Ireland. It was a fancy title for dictator. Cromwell was later offered the crown. But he refused because he believed in theocracy, not monarchy. Cromwell was perhaps emboldened by Hobbes' *Leviathan*. Under the theory of government articulated in *Leviathan*, a singularly powerful ruler like Cromwell was deemed legitimate so long as the people submitted to his rule. However, when Cromwell died in 1658, he left England without a legitimate government. So Parliament brought back the king.

The king hadn't forgotten about Cromwell's regicide in 1649. In fact, King Charles II was so angry at Cromwell for beheading his father that he had Cromwell's corpse exhumed, publicly hung, and beheaded. Cromwell's head was then mounted on the end of a wooden pole and displayed from the roof of Westminster Hall in London, along with the heads of his co-conspirators John Bradshaw and Henry Ireton, for more than twenty years. Eventually, the head was blown to the ground in a storm, where it was found by a guard. The guard took the head home and kept it for the rest of his life. In 1710, after the guard had died, his daughter sold the head to a private museum owner. And for the next hundred years, the head passed among private owners who put it on display in private museums and sideshows. But the head was a money-loser. So in 1815, the head was sold again, this time to a man named Josiah Henry Wilkinson. The head remained in the Wilkinson family until 1960, when one of Henry's descendants donated the head to Cromwell's alma mater, Sidney Sussex College at the University of Cambridge. On March 25, 1960, Sidney Sussex College took possession of the head where it remains to this day.

With Cromwell gone, Parliament restored the British monarchy in 1660. And after two more decades of conflict between Parliament and the monarchy, there was an event known as the

Glorious Revolution. Like the English Civil War, the Glorious Revolution was largely about religion. In 1688, a Protestant Parliament ousted King James II, who was a Catholic, and replaced him with the Protestant monarchs William and Mary from the Netherlands. But since King James II claimed to rule by a divine right from God, Parliament needed to justify its authority for removing him and crowning a new king. So in 1689, Parliament passed a law called the Bill of Rights and the newly crowned king William III signed it. By this piece of legislation, Parliament established that the institutions of the British government, including the monarchy, derived their respective powers from the consent of the British people. The divine right of English monarchs to rule over men finally was no more. From then on, English kings and queens would have to share power with Parliament, with the balance of power leaning in Parliament's favor.

Like his contemporary King Louis XIV of France, King James II was a double offender. He claimed to rule by divine right and he claimed absolute power as an absolute monarch. Thomas Hobbes did away with the divine right of kings and justified Parliament's actions in the wake of the English Civil War. But Hobbes remained a supporter of absolute monarchy. Now the Glorious Revolution needed a man who would do away with absolute monarchy as well and justify the new power-sharing arrangement between Parliament and William and Mary. That man was John Locke.

Like Thomas Hobbes, John Locke was a natural philosopher and empiricist who applied his knowledge in those areas to the study of man and government. Thus the same worldview which had been used to show beyond a doubt that the earth revolves around the sun was now being used to demonstrate that government is by the consent of the governed and that elected citizens make better rulers than kings. Locke learned natural philosophy and empiricism while he was a student at Oxford in the 1650s, where he was introduced to the new methods of Francis Bacon. Additionally, he was mentored by Robert Boyle who is known today for Boyle's Law, which describes the inverse relationship between the pressure and the volume of a gas. Locke was also an early member of the English Royal Society and later became acquainted with Isaac Newton and the esteemed Dutch mathematician and astronomer Christiaan Huygens. He earned his bachelor's degree from Oxford in 1656 and a master's degree in 1658. He also earned a degree in medicine in 1674. His most influential works *The Two Treatises of Government* and *An Essay Concerning Human Understanding* were published in 1689 and 1690, respectively. They form the basis of his thought on the social contract.

Locke accepted Hobbes' basic idea that government is by the consent of the governed. But for Locke, the consent of the governed meant more than merely acceding to the power of the sovereign in exchange for protection. He believed that mankind possessed the rational faculties and temperament to positively consent to the social contract. In other words, he believed people could govern themselves. Locke had a much more optimistic view of human nature than Hobbes, believing men were guided by natural reason and a desire to get along. He didn't believe that people were naturally good or bad. Holding fast to the empiricist tenet that all knowledge is derived from sense-experience, he believed every person was a blank slate at birth, a *tabula rasa*. In his view, human beings were the products of their experience. Consequently, the best citizens, leaders, and human beings, in his view, were formed in the crucible of self-determination, competition, and accountability that only a democratic society could provide.

Whereas Hobbes believed men had to surrender their liberty to a sovereign in exchange for peace and protection, Locke believed men should form limited governments and retain the bulk of their liberty for themselves. Whereas Hobbes advocated absolute monarchy, Locke advocated democracy. According to Locke, a king was no better than any other man and there were far more safeguards against tyranny in a democracy. But perhaps most importantly, the writings of John Locke would prove to have a tremendous influence on the founding fathers of the United States of America, the world's first and oldest constitutional democracy. And perhaps no founding father was more influenced by Locke than Thomas Jefferson. Anyone who thinks it is self-evident "that all men are created equal, that they are endowed by their Creator with certain unalienable Rights, that among these are Life, Liberty and the pursuit of Happiness" probably has John Locke to thank for it.

It is no exaggeration to say that from the time Martin Luther posted his ninety-five theses on the church door at Wittenberg in 1517 to the publication of John Locke's *The Two Treatises of Government* and *An Essay Concerning Human Understanding* in 1689 and 1690, respectively, the world witnessed the most significant development in government in the history of mankind. For thousands of years, Western civilization held to the belief that some men were divinely ordained to rule over other men. Even Athenian democracy was merely a transfer of this divine power from the aristocracy to all adult male citizens of Athens. Then, within the space of a mere two hundred years, everything changed. Mankind awoke to a new truth that government is created by men for the benefit of men. And within a century after the death of John Locke in 1704, the world would stand witness to the birth of the first constitutional democracy in human history, the United States of America.

And yet we assume this is the way things ought to be because each of us wears the worldview of Thomas Aquinas and John Duns Scotus and William of Ockham around our head like a halo. Only we don't know it. Of course we are born free; and of course government is by the consent of the governed; and of course all knowledge is derived from sense-experience; and of course objects tell us about nature, not God. These truths are self-evident only because that halo makes them so.

It started as a vision of heaven, infinite and eternal, in the mind of an African bishop who didn't know peace until he rested in God. Soon, however, the Word became flesh as the monks of Ireland endeavored to imitate Christ in body and mind. They built monasteries and schools and hospitals. They cared for the sick, comforted the poor, and educated countless generations. They did penance and followed Christ from earth to heaven, bringing forth an esthetic transformation of the Western mind that changed the world. They built a civilization like the sculptor who toils in silence to give voice to a stone. We wear their legacy like a halo. And even if many people today don't believe in God or Jesus Christ, we are free because they did.

Somewhere the Irish monks are smiling.

REFERENCES AND
SUGGESTED READING

Here are references for some of the quoted material in this book, as well as suggested reading for each chapter. In turn, many of the following books have excellent bibliographies or recommendations for further reading, which serve as superb guides to fascinating worlds. We have chosen to provide this information in lieu of endnotes or the kind of detailed bibliography that is often found in academic works because we believe it is more useful to the general reader.

1. HOW AN AFRICAN BISHOP
INVENTED EUROPE

St. Augustine's own words in this chapter come from his *Confessions*, of which there are many fine translations. We recommend reading it aloud as Augustine intended, perhaps in a group setting. If you're looking for a biography of Augustine, one of the best is Peter Brown's *Augustine of Hippo*. We also recommend Augustine's *City of God* and his *Enchiridion on Faith, Hope, and Love*. Additionally, there are very good sources for Pelagius. Two that we recommend are *Pelagius: Life and Letters* by B.R. Rees and *Pelagius's Commentary on St. Paul's Epistle to the Romans* by Theodore De Bruyn.

2. A SLAVE IN IRELAND SOWS
THE SEED OF A NEW CIVILIZATION

Of St. Patrick's writings, copies of only two letters survive. They are his *Confession* and his *Letter to the Soldiers of Coroticus.* Both are short, available in translation, and well worth the small investment of time to read. The quotations attributed to Patrick in this chapter are from his *Confession.* For an expertly written biography of Patrick, we suggest Philip Freeman's *St. Patrick of Ireland.* Also, we strongly recommend *Early Christian Ireland* by T.M. Charles-Edwards for a comprehensive and scholarly study of Irish civilization during this era.

3. THE SECRET GOSPEL OF IRELAND

Finnian's penitential quoted in this chapter is from *Medieval Handbooks of Penance,* translated by John McNeil and Helena Gamer. For further reading on John Cassian, try *Cassian the Monk* by Columba Stewart. There are many good books on early Christian Ireland. Again, we recommend *Early Christian Ireland* by T.M. Charles-Edwards, as well as *Early Medieval Ireland* by Dáibhí Ó Cróinín. For more on the Irish Church, read *Celtic Theology* by Thomas O'Loughlin. As for the story of Columba, Adomnán's *Life of St. Columba* is where it all begins. Finally, pick up a copy of Liam de Paor's *Saint Patrick's World* for analysis and a fine compilation of extracts from select historical documents of the age.

4. HOW THE IRISH INVADED EUROPE

The original story of St. Columbanus comes from Jonas of Susa's *Life of St. Columbanus.* For a scholarly treatment of Columbanus and the sources, *Early Christian Ireland* by T.M.

Charles-Edwards is second to none. But perhaps the most entertaining and lyrical telling of Columbanus' life is *Saint Columban* by the Irish writer Francis MacManus. As for John Scotus Eriugena, he is a rather tough nut to crack. His masterwork is *Periphyseon*. However, we recommend reading *John Scotus Eriugena* by Deirdre Carabine before attempting to read *Periphyseon*. We also recommend *The Philosophy of John Scouts Eriugena: A Study of Idealism in the Middle Ages* by Dermot Moran.

5. IRISH CHRISTIANITY AND THE THREE WISE MEN

The first biographies of St. Thomas Aquinas all date to the early fourteenth century. They are *Life of St. Thomas* by Peter Calo, *Life of St. Thomas Aquinas* by William of Tocco, *St. Thomas Aquinas* by Bartolommeo of Lucca, and *Life of St. Thomas* by Bernard Gui. For an excellent twentieth-century rendering of the saint's life, we recommend *Saint Thomas Aquinas: The Dumb Ox* by G.K. Chesterton. As for Thomas Aquinas' philosophy and theology, F.C. Copleston provides a very good introduction to the subject in *Aquinas: An Introduction to the Life and Work of the Great Medieval Thinker*. However, we highly recommend starting with *Aquinas 101* by Francis Selman. There are many good books on John Duns Scotus. For a superb introduction to the man and his thought, try *Scotus for Dunces: An Introduction to the Subtle Doctor* by Mary Beth Ingham. And finally, a nice place to start for a modern introduction to William of Ockham is Rondo Keele's *Ockham Explained: From Razor to Rebellion*.

6. THE HIDDEN LEGACY OF
IRISH CHRISTIANITY

A splendid biography of Martin Luther is Roland Bainton's *Here I Stand: A Life of Martin Luther*. For an accessible window into the life and thought of John Calvin, try W. Robert Godfrey's reverential *John Calvin: Pilgrim and Pastor*. As for Oliver Cromwell, we suggest *Oliver Cromwell: God's Warrior and the English Revolution* by I.J. Gentles, *Oliver Cromwell: Politics and Religion in the English Revolution 1640-1658* by David L. Smith, and *Cromwell's Head* by Jonathan Fitzgibbons. Lastly, for a general history of Britain, *The Oxford History of Britain* makes a fine addition to any library.

INDEX

Viterbo, 146
Vosges Mountains, 99, 104
Vulgate, 43

W
Wartburg Castle, 186, 188
Western Europe, 46, 48, 65, 72-
    73, 85-86, 103-104, 118-122,
    124, 131, 134, 173, 180
Western Roman Empire, 46, 77
Westminster Hall, 206
Whittingham, William, 197
Wilfrid, 94-96, 98, 106-107
Wilkinson, Josiah Henry, 206
William and Mary, 207
William of St. Amour, 144-145
Wycliffe, John, 167

Z
Zurich, 114, 193-194
Zwingli, Ulrich, 192-194, 197

19123172R10135

Made in the USA
Lexington, KY
07 December 2012